AMINATION SERIES

D0339832

THIS IS YOUR **PASSBOOK**® FOR ...

POSTAL ENTRANCE BATTERY TEST (473)

NATIONAL LEARNING CORPORATION®
passbooks.com

PASSBOOK® SERIES

THE *PASSBOOK® SERIES* has been created to prepare applicants and candidates for the ultimate academic battlefield – the examination room.

At some time in our lives, each and every one of us may be required to take an examination – for validation, matriculation, admission, qualification, registration, certification, or licensure.

Based on the assumption that every applicant or candidate has met the basic formal educational standards, has taken the required number of courses, and read the necessary texts, the *PASSBOOK® SERIES* furnishes the one special preparation which may assure passing with confidence, instead of failing with insecurity. Examination questions – together with answers – are furnished as the basic vehicle for study so that the mysteries of the examination and its compounding difficulties may be eliminated or diminished by a sure method.

This book is meant to help you pass your examination provided that you qualify and are serious in your objective.

The entire field is reviewed through the huge store of content information which is succinctly presented through a provocative and challenging approach – the question-and-answer method.

A climate of success is established by furnishing the correct answers at the end of each test.

You soon learn to recognize types of questions, forms of questions, and patterns of questioning. You may even begin to anticipate expected outcomes.

You perceive that many questions are repeated or adapted so that you can gain acute insights, which may enable you to score many sure points.

You learn how to confront new questions, or types of questions, and to attack them confidently and work out the correct answers.

You note objectives and emphases, and recognize pitfalls and dangers, so that you may make positive educational adjustments.

Moreover, you are kept fully informed in relation to new concepts, methods, practices, and directions in the field.

You discover that you arre actually taking the examination all the time: you are preparing for the examination by "taking" an examination, not by reading extraneous and/or supererogatory textbooks.

In short, this PASSBOOK®, used directedly, should be an important factor in helping you to pass your test.

POSTAL ENTRANCE BATTERY TEST #473

The Postal Battery Test #473 is an official entrance examination of the United States Postal Service for the following positions:

> City Carrier
> Mail Processing Clerk
> Mail Handler
> Sales, Services and Distribution Associate

Hundreds of positions are expected to be filled based on the results of the examination. All hires will start as part-time flexible workers before gaining regular full-time posts.

Part-time flexible employees are not guaranteed 40 hours of work a week and must work irregular hours. generally, they become regular full-time employees, with holidays off, after six months.

City Carriers collect and deliver mail either on foot or by vehicle, and the position requires prolonged standing, walking and the ability to carry mailbags weighing 35 pounds and to lift up to 70 pounds.

Mail Processing Clerks monitor the performance of both automated processing equipment and manual mail sorting. Handlers load, unload and transport mail containers and equipment. Mail Handlers must be able to lift, carry and push up to 70 pounds of mail.

Sales, Services and Distribution Associates must complete an on-the-job training program before filling their position as a sales and service representative as well as a mail distributor.

Applicants for these jobs must meet the general age and citizenship requirements. Certain jobs also have additional requirements. For positions requiring driving, applicants must have a state driver's license and a safe driving record. Applicants must have vision of 20/40 in one eye and the ability to read without strain regular printed material, glasses permitted.

EXAMINATION

The written exam will test literary and basic clerical skills. Applicants will be examined on a first-come, first-served basis. The exam and completion of required forms will require approximately two hours and 15 minutes. At the time of the examination, the applicant may select his or her preference of all four jobs.

Those persons who pass the written exam must also pass a drug test, and candidates for certain jobs also just pass a job-simulated performance exercise or other test.

The following chart breaks down the sections of the test along with an overview of the subject matter and the ie allotted:

Section	Brief Overview	Time / Items / Notes
Part A Address Checking	Tests the ability to compare two lists of information in order to determine if there are any discrepancies and, if so, the ability to identify where the errors occur.	11 minutes / 60 items *Random guessing is not advised since wrong answers will be penalized*
Part B Forms Completion	The applicant will be given blank sample forms commonly used by the Postal Service and tested on the ability to identify the information that would correctly complete the necessary forms.	15 minutes / 30 items *Guessing is advised since wrong answers will NOT be penalized*
Part C Section 1 - Coding	Tests the ability to accurately assign the proper code letters to the corresponding range of addresses in a short amount of time.	6 minutes / 36 items *Wrong answers will be penalized*
Part C Section 2 - Memory	Same as Coding section except answers must be given based on memorization of previously-used code guide. You will not have access to the guide in this section.	7 minutes / 36 items *Wrong answers will be penalized*
Part D Personal Characteristics and Experience Inventory	This section assesses the applicant's suitability for employment with the Postal Service based on answers to questions of character, personal tendencies and experience.	90 minutes / 236 items

WHAT IS THIS BOOK   ALL ABOUT?

This book   will give you a good idea of what you have to do when you take the Civil Service tests for jobs in the Post Office.

—It shows how to apply for the test.

—It explains how to do the different kinds of questions.

—It describes how to mark your answers on the answer sheet.

—It gives some of each kind of question to try.

—Finally, it gives you a chance to test yourself with tests just like those used in the examination—same kinds of questions, same difficulty, same length.

The material is arranged so that you can study by yourself. Read the explanation, try the questions, check your answers. For the questions you get wrong, try to figure out why the correct answer is right and why you made a mistake. If you are working by yourself and you can't figure out why the correct answer is right, try to get some help. Ask a teacher; a librarian; perhaps a brother, a sister, or friend who has gone to high school.

SO YOU WANT TO WORK FOR THE POST OFFICE

THAT'S GREAT!

But...Did You Know

- You have to be 18 or over
  (16 if you are a high school graduate)
- You have to pass a physical examination
- You have to be a United States citizen
- YOU HAVE TO PASS A CIVIL SERVICE TEST

You will find in this book   tests that are very much like the tests you have to take to get a job in the Post Office.

READ AND STUDY THIS BOOK   CAREFULLY.

HERE ARE SOME POST OFFICE JOBS

- You could be a MAIL HANDLER.
  You would help move the mail (it's heavy) within the Post Office building.

- You could be a DISTRIBUTION CLERK.
  You would sort the mail (in some places by hand, in some places by machine) and do other things to keep the mail moving.

- You could be a MAIL CARRIER.
  You would deliver mail to homes, stores, and offices.

YOU MUST TAKE AND PASS A CIVIL SERVICE TEST IN ORDER TO BE HIRED FOR ANY OF THESE JOBS.

(There are sometimes openings for DRIVERS and GARAGEMEN.
There are not many of these jobs, but it's worth checking with your local Post Office or the Federal Job Information Center if you're interested.)

How Do You Apply for a Post Office Job?

FIRST: Go to your nearest Post Office or Federal Job Information Center. Tell them you want to apply for a Post Office job. You will get a form to fill out.

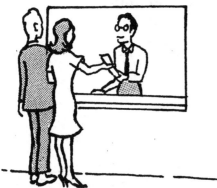

(If they are not accepting applications now, find out when they expect to accept them again. It might be a good idea to start getting ready for the examination anyway.)

You can find the address of your nearest Post Office or Federal Job Information Center in the telephone book.

When you get this form, be sure to find out WHEN you have to send it in, and WHERE you send it.

SECOND: Look over the form. If you don't know how to answer all the questions, ask someone in the office or someone you know for help. If there is no one to help you,

- Answer all the questions the best you can.
- Be sure to print your name and address.

This is what the Application Form looks like

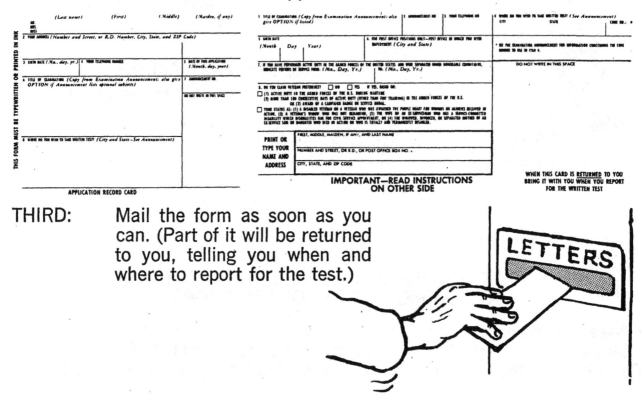

THIRD: Mail the form as soon as you can. (Part of it will be returned to you, telling you when and where to report for the test.)

After You Send in Your Application Form

You have mailed in your application form. Soon, you will get back the part that tells you when and where to take the Civil Service test. This is called your admission card. It looks like this:

1. TITLE OF EXAMINATION (Copy from Examination Announcement; also give OPTION if listed)	2. ANNOUNCEMENT NO.	3. YOUR TELEPHONE NO.	4. WHERE DO YOU WISH TO TAKE WRITTEN TEST? (See Announcement) CITY: STATE: CODE NO.: *
5. BIRTH DATE (Month Day Year)	6. FOR POST OFFICE POSITIONS ONLY—POST OFFICE IN WHICH YOU WISH EMPLOYMENT (City and State)		* SEE THE EXAMINATION ANNOUNCEMENT FOR INFORMATION CONCERNING THE CODE NUMBER TO USE IN ITEM 4.

7. IF YOU HAVE PERFORMED ACTIVE DUTY IN THE ARMED FORCES OF THE UNITED STATES AND WERE SEPARATED UNDER HONORABLE CONDITIONS, INDICATE PERIODS OF SERVICE FROM: (Mo., Day, Yr.)   TO: (Mo., Day, Yr.)

DO NOT WRITE IN THIS SPACE

8. DO YOU CLAIM VETERAN PREFERENCE? ☐ NO ☐ YES IF YES, BASED ON:
☐ (1) ACTIVE DUTY IN THE ARMED FORCES OF THE U.S. DURING WARTIME
(2) MORE THAN 180 CONSECUTIVE DAYS OF ACTIVE DUTY (OTHER THAN FOR TRAINING) IN THE ARMED FORCES OF THE U.S.
OR (3) AWARD OF A CAMPAIGN BADGE OR SERVICE MEDAL.
☐ YOUR STATUS AS: (1) A DISABLED VETERAN OR A VETERAN WHO WAS AWARDED THE PURPLE HEART FOR WOUNDS OR INJURIES RECEIVED IN ACTION, (2) A VETERAN'S WIDOW WHO HAS NOT REMARRIED, (3) THE WIFE OF AN EX-SERVICEMAN WHO HAS A SERVICE-CONNECTED DISABILITY WHICH DISQUALIFIES HIM FOR CIVIL SERVICE APPOINTMENT, OR (4) THE WIDOWED, DIVORCED, OR SEPARATED MOTHER OF AN EX-SERVICE SON OR DAUGHTER WHO DIED IN ACTION OR WHO IS TOTALLY AND PERMANENTLY DISABLED.

You will be told here where and when to report for your test.

PRINT OR TYPE YOUR NAME AND ADDRESS

FIRST, MIDDLE, MAIDEN, IF ANY, AND LAST NAME

NUMBER AND STREET, OR R.D., OR POST OFFICE BOX NO.

CITY, STATE, AND ZIP CODE

IMPORTANT—READ INSTRUCTIONS ON OTHER SIDE

WHEN THIS CARD IS RETURNED TO YOU BRING IT WITH YOU WHEN YOU REPORT FOR THE WRITTEN TEST

Of course, if you did not put down your correct address, or if you forgot to put in your name, you will not hear from anybody.

DO IT RIGHT.

. . . DON'T GET JITTERY JUST BECAUSE
YOU HAVE TO TAKE A TEST.

Go over the tests in this book   as carefully as you can.
This will help you get ready to take the real test.

AND REMEMBER WHEN YOU SHOW UP

- **Be Sure You Have Had
A Good Night's Sleep**

- **Be On Time**

- **Bring Your Admission Card**

IF YOU FORGET TO BRING YOUR ADMISSION CARD, YOU WILL
HAVE TO COME BACK ANOTHER TIME, DON'T FORGET

GOOD LUCK...

HOW TO MARK YOUR ANSWER SHEET

The Answer Sheet is where you mark your answers. Your score on the test depends on the marks you make on your Answer Sheet. Therefore, you must mark it exactly the way you are told in the examination room. Some advice on how to use the Answer Sheet is given on this page.

On the next page, you see what a whole Answer Sheet looks like.
Notice how the numbers on the Answer Sheet run across the page—like this:

Your answer mark should look LIKE THIS ——▶
A neat, heavy line, inside the box.

Do NOT mark your answers like this ——▶ ✗ or ⊕ or ✗ or ▓

Don't take a long time to make your marks. Make a heavy pencil mark and move on to the next question.

For practice, mark the boxes for the following number-letter combinations on the Answer Sheet on the next page. The first four in PART A have been done to show how; you do the rest of PART A—

PART A—1A 2A 3D 4A 5D 6A 7D 8A 9A 10D 11D
12A 13A 14A 15D 16D

Now mark the boxes for the following number-letter combinations in PART B.

PART B—1B 2C 3A 4D 5E 6E 7A 8E 9D 10D 11B
12C 13C 14D 15E

TEST NO. _____	EXAMINING OFFICE CODE			IDENTIFICATION NO.	DO NOT WRITE IN THIS BOX
SERIES NO. _____	PRINT NAME _____				0 1 2 3 4 5 6 7 8

(Last)   (First)   (M.I.)

ADDRESS _____

(NUMBER)   (STREET)

BIRTH DATE _____

DO NOT WRITE IN THIS BOX

(CITY)   (STATE)   (ZIP CODE)

ANSWER SHEET

PART A

1 2 3 4 5 6 7 8 9 10 11 12 13 14 15
16 17 18 19 20 21 22 23 24 25 26 27 28 29 30 31
32 33 34 35 36 37 38 39 40 41 42 43 44 45 46 47
48 49 50 51 52 53 54 55 56 57 58 59 60 61 62 63
64 65 66 67 68 69 70 71 72 73 74 75 76 77 78 79
80 81 82 83 84 85 86 87 88 89 90 91 92 93 94 95

PART B

1 2 3 4 5 6 7 8
9 10 11 12 13 14 15 16
17 18 19 20 21 22 23 24
25 26 27 28 29 30 31 32
33 34 35 36 37 38 39 40
41 42 43 44 45 46 47 48
49 50 51 52 53 54 55 56
57 58 59 60 61 62 63 64
65 66 67 68 69 70 71 72
73 74 75 76 77 78 79 80
81 82 83 84 85 86 87 88

SIGNATURE _____
Stray marks may be counted as errors.
Erase COMPLETELY all marks except your answers.

PART C

1 2 3 4 5 6 7 8
9 10 11 12 13 14 15 16
17 18 19 20 21 22 23 24
25 26 27 28 29 30 31 32

PART D

1 2 3 4 5 6 7 8
9 10 11 12 13 14 15 16
17 18 19 20 21 22 23 24

HOW TO TAKE A TEST

I. YOU MUST PASS AN EXAMINATION

A. *WHAT EVERY CANDIDATE SHOULD KNOW*

Examination applicants often ask us for help in preparing for the written test. What can I study in advance? What kinds of questions will be asked? How will the test be given? How will the papers be graded?

As an applicant for a civil service examination, you may be wondering about some of these things. Our purpose here is to suggest effective methods of advance study and to describe civil service examinations.

Your chances for success on this examination can be increased if you know how to prepare. Those "pre-examination jitters" can be reduced if you know what to expect. You can even experience an adventure in good citizenship if you know why civil service exams are given.

B. *WHY ARE CIVIL SERVICE EXAMINATIONS GIVEN?*

Civil service examinations are important to you in two ways. As a citizen, you want public jobs filled by employees who know how to do their work. As a job seeker, you want a fair chance to compete for that job on an equal footing with other candidates. The best-known means of accomplishing this two-fold goal is the competitive examination.

Exams are widely publicized throughout the nation. They may be administered for jobs in federal, state, city, municipal, town or village governments or agencies.

Any citizen may apply, with some limitations, such as the age or residence of applicants. Your experience and education may be reviewed to see whether you meet the requirements for the particular examination. When these requirements exist, they are reasonable and applied consistently to all applicants. Thus, a competitive examination may cause you some uneasiness now, but it is your privilege and safeguard.

C. *HOW ARE CIVIL SERVICE EXAMS DEVELOPED?*

Examinations are carefully written by trained technicians who are specialists in the field known as "psychological measurement," in consultation with recognized authorities in the field of work that the test will cover. These experts recommend the subject matter areas or skills to be tested; only those knowledges or skills important to your success on the job are included. The most reliable books and source materials available are used as references. Together, the experts and technicians judge the difficulty level of the questions.

Test technicians know how to phrase questions so that the problem is clearly stated. Their ethics do not permit "trick" or "catch" questions. Questions may have been tried out on sample groups, or subjected to statistical analysis, to determine their usefulness.

Written tests are often used in combination with performance tests, ratings of training and experience, and oral interviews. All of these measures combine to form the best-known means of finding the right person for the right job.

II. HOW TO PASS THE WRITTEN TEST

A. *NATURE OF THE EXAMINATION*

To prepare intelligently for civil service examinations, you should know how they differ from school examinations you have taken. In school you were assigned certain definite pages to read or subjects to cover. The examination questions were quite detailed and usually emphasized memory. Civil service exams, on the other hand, try to discover your present ability to perform the duties of a position, plus your potentiality to learn these duties. In other words, a civil service exam attempts to predict how successful you will be. Questions cover such a broad area that they cannot be as minute and detailed as school exam questions.

In the public service similar kinds of work, or positions, are grouped together in one "class." This process is known as *position-classification*. All the positions in a class are paid according to the salary range for that class. One class title covers all of these positions, and they are all tested by the same examination.

B. *FOUR BASIC STEPS*

1) Study the announcement

How, then, can you know what subjects to study? Our best answer is: "Learn as much as possible about the class of positions for which you've applied." The exam will test the knowledge, skills and abilities needed to do the work.

Your most valuable source of information about the position you want is the official exam announcement. This announcement lists the training and experience qualifications. Check these standards and apply only if you come reasonably close to meeting them.

The brief description of the position in the examination announcement offers some clues to the subjects which will be tested. Think about the job itself. Review the duties in your mind. Can you perform them, or are there some in which you are rusty? Fill in the blank spots in your preparation.

Many jurisdictions preview the written test in the exam announcement by including a section called "Knowledge and Abilities Required," "Scope of the Examination," or some similar heading. Here you will find out specifically what fields will be tested.

2) Review your own background

Once you learn in general what the position is all about, and what you need to know to do the work, ask yourself which subjects you already know fairly well and which need improvement. You may wonder whether to concentrate on improving your strong areas or on building some background in your fields of weakness. When the announcement has specified "some knowledge" or "considerable knowledge," or has used adjectives like "beginning principles of..." or "advanced ... methods," you can get a clue as to the number and difficulty of questions to be asked in any given field. More questions, and hence broader coverage, would be included for those subjects which are more important in the work. Now weigh your strengths and weaknesses against the job requirements and prepare accordingly.

3) Determine the level of the position

      Another way to tell how intensively you should prepare is to understand the level of the job for which you are applying. Is it the entering level? In other words, is this the position in which beginners in a field of work are hired? Or is it an intermediate or advanced level? Sometimes this is indicated by such words as "Junior" or "Senior" in the class title. Other jurisdictions use Roman numerals to designate the level – Clerk I, Clerk II, for example. The word "Supervisor" sometimes appears in the title. If the level is not indicated by the title, check the description of duties. Will you be working under very close supervision, or will you have responsibility for independent decisions in this work?

4) Choose appropriate study materials

      Now that you know the subjects to be examined and the relative amount of each subject to be covered, you can choose suitable study materials. For beginning level jobs, or even advanced ones, if you have a pronounced weakness in some aspect of your training, read a modern, standard textbook in that field. Be sure it is up to date and has general coverage. Such books are normally available at your library, and the librarian will be glad to help you locate one. For entry-level positions, questions of appropriate difficulty are chosen – neither highly advanced questions, nor those too simple. Such questions require careful thought but not advanced training.

      If the position for which you are applying is technical or advanced, you will read more advanced, specialized material. If you are already familiar with the basic principles of your field, elementary textbooks would waste your time. Concentrate on advanced textbooks and technical periodicals. Think through the concepts and review difficult problems in your field.

      These are all general sources. You can get more ideas on your own initiative, following these leads. For example, training manuals and publications of the government agency which employs workers in your field can be useful, particularly for technical and professional positions. A letter or visit to the government department involved may result in more specific study suggestions, and certainly will provide you with a more definite idea of the exact nature of the position you are seeking.

III. KINDS OF TESTS

      Tests are used for purposes other than measuring knowledge and ability to perform specified duties. For some positions, it is equally important to test ability to make adjustments to new situations or to profit from training. In others, basic mental abilities not dependent on information are essential. Questions which test these things may not appear as pertinent to the duties of the position as those which test for knowledge and information. Yet they are often highly important parts of a fair examination. For very general questions, it is almost impossible to help you direct your study efforts. What we can do is to point out some of the more common of these general abilities needed in public service positions and describe some typical questions.

1) General information

      Broad, general information has been found useful for predicting job success in some kinds of work. This is tested in a variety of ways, from vocabulary lists to questions about current events. Basic background in some field of work, such as sociology or economics, may be sampled in a group of questions. Often these are principles which have become familiar to most persons through exposure rather than through formal training. It is difficult to advise you how to study for these questions; being alert to the world around you is our best suggestion.

2) Verbal ability

An example of an ability needed in many positions is verbal or language ability. Verbal ability is, in brief, the ability to use and understand words. Vocabulary and grammar tests are typical measures of this ability. Reading comprehension or paragraph interpretation questions are common in many kinds of civil service tests. You are given a paragraph of written material and asked to find its central meaning.

3) Numerical ability

Number skills can be tested by the familiar arithmetic problem, by checking paired lists of numbers to see which are alike and which are different, or by interpreting charts and graphs. In the latter test, a graph may be printed in the test booklet which you are asked to use as the basis for answering questions.

4) Observation

A popular test for law-enforcement positions is the observation test. A picture is shown to you for several minutes, then taken away. Questions about the picture test your ability to observe both details and larger elements.

5) Following directions

In many positions in the public service, the employee must be able to carry out written instructions dependably and accurately. You may be given a chart with several columns, each column listing a variety of information. The questions require you to carry out directions involving the information given in the chart.

6) Skills and aptitudes

Performance tests effectively measure some manual skills and aptitudes. When the skill is one in which you are trained, such as typing or shorthand, you can practice. These tests are often very much like those given in business school or high school courses. For many of the other skills and aptitudes, however, no short-time preparation can be made. Skills and abilities natural to you or that you have developed throughout your lifetime are being tested.

Many of the general questions just described provide all the data needed to answer the questions and ask you to use your reasoning ability to find the answers. Your best preparation for these tests, as well as for tests of facts and ideas, is to be at your physical and mental best. You, no doubt, have your own methods of getting into an exam-taking mood and keeping "in shape." The next section lists some ideas on this subject.

IV. KINDS OF QUESTIONS

Only rarely is the "essay" question, which you answer in narrative form, used in civil service tests. Civil service tests are usually of the short-answer type. Full instructions for answering these questions will be given to you at the examination. But in case this is your first experience with short-answer questions and separate answer sheets, here is what you need to know:

1) Multiple-choice Questions

Most popular of the short-answer questions is the "multiple choice" or "best answer" question. It can be used, for example, to test for factual knowledge, ability to solve problems or judgment in meeting situations found at work.

A multiple-choice question is normally one of three types—

- It can begin with an incomplete statement followed by several possible endings. You are to find the one ending which *best* completes the statement, although some of the others may not be entirely wrong.
- It can also be a complete statement in the form of a question which is answered by choosing one of the statements listed.
- It can be in the form of a problem – again you select the best answer.

Here is an example of a multiple-choice question with a discussion which should give you some clues as to the method for choosing the right answer:

When an employee has a complaint about his assignment, the action which will *best* help him overcome his difficulty is to
  A. discuss his difficulty with his coworkers
  B. take the problem to the head of the organization
  C. take the problem to the person who gave him the assignment
  D. say nothing to anyone about his complaint

In answering this question, you should study each of the choices to find which is best. Consider choice "A" – Certainly an employee may discuss his complaint with fellow employees, but no change or improvement can result, and the complaint remains unresolved. Choice "B" is a poor choice since the head of the organization probably does not know what assignment you have been given, and taking your problem to him is known as "going over the head" of the supervisor. The supervisor, or person who made the assignment, is the person who can clarify it or correct any injustice. Choice "C" is, therefore, correct. To say nothing, as in choice "D," is unwise. Supervisors have and interest in knowing the problems employees are facing, and the employee is seeking a solution to his problem.

2) True/False Questions

The "true/false" or "right/wrong" form of question is sometimes used. Here a complete statement is given. Your job is to decide whether the statement is right or wrong.

SAMPLE: A roaming cell-phone call to a nearby city costs less than a non-roaming call to a distant city.

This statement is wrong, or false, since roaming calls are more expensive.
This is not a complete list of all possible question forms, although most of the others are variations of these common types. You will always get complete directions for

answering questions. Be sure you understand *how* to mark your answers – ask questions until you do.

V. RECORDING YOUR ANSWERS

Computer terminals are used more and more today for many different kinds of exams.

For an examination with very few applicants, you may be told to record your answers in the test booklet itself. Separate answer sheets are much more common. If this separate answer sheet is to be scored by machine – and this is often the case – it is highly important that you mark your answers correctly in order to get credit.

An electronic scoring machine is often used in civil service offices because of the speed with which papers can be scored. Machine-scored answer sheets must be marked with a pencil, which will be given to you. This pencil has a high graphite content which responds to the electronic scoring machine. As a matter of fact, stray dots may register as answers, so do not let your pencil rest on the answer sheet while you are pondering the correct answer. Also, if your pencil lead breaks or is otherwise defective, ask for another.

Since the answer sheet will be dropped in a slot in the scoring machine, be careful not to bend the corners or get the paper crumpled.

The answer sheet normally has five vertical columns of numbers, with 30 numbers to a column. These numbers correspond to the question numbers in your test booklet. After each number, going across the page are four or five pairs of dotted lines. These short dotted lines have small letters or numbers above them. The first two pairs may also have a "T" or "F" above the letters. This indicates that the first two pairs only are to be used if the questions are of the true-false type. If the questions are multiple choice, disregard the "T" and "F" and pay attention only to the small letters or numbers.

Answer your questions in the manner of the sample that follows:

32. The largest city in the United States is
    A. Washington, D.C.
    B. New York City
    C. Chicago
    D. Detroit
    E. San Francisco

1) Choose the answer you think is best. (New York City is the largest, so "B" is correct.)
2) Find the row of dotted lines numbered the same as the question you are answering. (Find row number 32)
3) Find the pair of dotted lines corresponding to the answer. (Find the pair of lines under the mark "B.")
4) Make a solid black mark between the dotted lines.

VI. BEFORE THE TEST

Common sense will help you find procedures to follow to get ready for an examination. Too many of us, however, overlook these sensible measures. Indeed, nervousness and fatigue have been found to be the most serious reasons why applicants fail to do their best on civil service tests. Here is a list of reminders:

- Begin your preparation early – Don't wait until the last minute to go scurrying around for books and materials or to find out what the position is all about.
- Prepare continuously – An hour a night for a week is better than an all-night cram session. This has been definitely established. What is more, a night a week for a month will return better dividends than crowding your study into a shorter period of time.
- Locate the place of the exam – You have been sent a notice telling you when and where to report for the examination. If the location is in a different town or otherwise unfamiliar to you, it would be well to inquire the best route and learn something about the building.
- Relax the night before the test – Allow your mind to rest. Do not study at all that night. Plan some mild recreation or diversion; then go to bed early and get a good night's sleep.
- Get up early enough to make a leisurely trip to the place for the test – This way unforeseen events, traffic snarls, unfamiliar buildings, etc. will not upset you.
- Dress comfortably – A written test is not a fashion show. You will be known by number and not by name, so wear something comfortable.
- Leave excess paraphernalia at home – Shopping bags and odd bundles will get in your way. You need bring only the items mentioned in the official notice you received; usually everything you need is provided. Do not bring reference books to the exam. They will only confuse those last minutes and be taken away from you when in the test room.
- Arrive somewhat ahead of time – If because of transportation schedules you must get there very early, bring a newspaper or magazine to take your mind off yourself while waiting.
- Locate the examination room – When you have found the proper room, you will be directed to the seat or part of the room where you will sit. Sometimes you are given a sheet of instructions to read while you are waiting. Do not fill out any forms until you are told to do so; just read them and be prepared.
- Relax and prepare to listen to the instructions
- If you have any physical problem that may keep you from doing your best, be sure to tell the test administrator. If you are sick or in poor health, you really cannot do your best on the exam. You can come back and take the test some other time.

VII. AT THE TEST

The day of the test is here and you have the test booklet in your hand. The temptation to get going is very strong. Caution! There is more to success than knowing the right answers. You must know how to identify your papers and understand variations in the type of short-answer question used in this particular examination. Follow these suggestions for maximum results from your efforts:

1) Cooperate with the monitor

The test administrator has a duty to create a situation in which you can be as much at ease as possible. He will give instructions, tell you when to begin, check to see that you are marking your answer sheet correctly, and so on. He is not there to guard you, although he will see that your competitors do not take unfair advantage. He wants to help you do your best.

2) Listen to all instructions

Don't jump the gun! Wait until you understand all directions. In most civil service tests you get more time than you need to answer the questions. So don't be in a hurry. Read each word of instructions until you clearly understand the meaning. Study the examples, listen to all announcements and follow directions. Ask questions if you do not understand what to do.

3) Identify your papers

Civil service exams are usually identified by number only. You will be assigned a number; you must not put your name on your test papers. Be sure to copy your number correctly. Since more than one exam may be given, copy your exact examination title.

4) Plan your time

Unless you are told that a test is a "speed" or "rate of work" test, speed itself is usually not important. Time enough to answer all the questions will be provided, but this does not mean that you have all day. An overall time limit has been set. Divide the total time (in minutes) by the number of questions to determine the approximate time you have for each question.

5) Do not linger over difficult questions

If you come across a difficult question, mark it with a paper clip (useful to have along) and come back to it when you have been through the booklet. One caution if you do this – be sure to skip a number on your answer sheet as well. Check often to be sure that you have not lost your place and that you are marking in the row numbered the same as the question you are answering.

6) Read the questions

Be sure you know what the question asks! Many capable people are unsuccessful because they failed to *read* the questions correctly.

7) Answer all questions

Unless you have been instructed that a penalty will be deducted for incorrect answers, it is better to guess than to omit a question.

8) Speed tests

It is often better NOT to guess on speed tests. It has been found that on timed tests people are tempted to spend the last few seconds before time is called in marking answers at random – without even reading them – in the hope of picking up a few extra points. To discourage this practice, the instructions may warn you that your score will be "corrected" for guessing. That is, a penalty will be applied. The incorrect answers will be deducted from the correct ones, or some other penalty formula will be used.

9) Review your answers

   If you finish before time is called, go back to the questions you guessed or omitted to give them further thought. Review other answers if you have time.

10) Return your test materials

   If you are ready to leave before others have finished or time is called, take ALL your materials to the monitor and leave quietly. Never take any test material with you. The monitor can discover whose papers are not complete, and taking a test booklet may be grounds for disqualification.

VIII. EXAMINATION TECHNIQUES

1) Read the general instructions carefully. These are usually printed on the first page of the exam booklet. As a rule, these instructions refer to the timing of the examination; the fact that you should not start work until the signal and must stop work at a signal, etc. If there are any *special* instructions, such as a choice of questions to be answered, make sure that you note this instruction carefully.

2) When you are ready to start work on the examination, that is as soon as the signal has been given, read the instructions to each question booklet, underline any key words or phrases, such as *least, best, outline, describe* and the like. In this way you will tend to answer as requested rather than discover on reviewing your paper that you *listed without describing*, that you selected the *worst* choice rather than the *best* choice, etc.

3) If the examination is of the objective or multiple-choice type – that is, each question will also give a series of possible answers: A, B, C or D, and you are called upon to select the best answer and write the letter next to that answer on your answer paper – it is advisable to start answering each question in turn. There may be anywhere from 50 to 100 such questions in the three or four hours allotted and you can see how much time would be taken if you read through all the questions before beginning to answer any. Furthermore, if you come across a question or group of questions which you know would be difficult to answer, it would undoubtedly affect your handling of all the other questions.

4) If the examination is of the essay type and contains but a few questions, it is a moot point as to whether you should read all the questions before starting to answer any one. Of course, if you are given a choice – say five out of seven and the like – then it is essential to read all the questions so you can eliminate the two that are most difficult. If, however, you are asked to answer all the questions, there may be danger in trying to answer the easiest one first because you may find that you will spend too much time on it. The best technique is to answer the first question, then proceed to the second, etc.

5) Time your answers. Before the exam begins, write down the time it started, then add the time allowed for the examination and write down the time it must be completed, then divide the time available somewhat as follows:

- If 3-1/2 hours are allowed, that would be 210 minutes. If you have 80 objective-type questions, that would be an average of 2-1/2 minutes per question. Allow yourself no more than 2 minutes per question, or a total of 160 minutes, which will permit about 50 minutes to review.
- If for the time allotment of 210 minutes there are 7 essay questions to answer, that would average about 30 minutes a question. Give yourself only 25 minutes per question so that you have about 35 minutes to review.

6) The most important instruction is to *read each question* and make sure you know what is wanted. The second most important instruction is to *time yourself properly* so that you answer every question. The third most important instruction is to *answer every question*. Guess if you have to but include something for each question. Remember that you will receive no credit for a blank and will probably receive some credit if you write something in answer to an essay question. If you guess a letter – say "B" for a multiple-choice question – you may have guessed right. If you leave a blank as an answer to a multiple-choice question, the examiners may respect your feelings but it will not add a point to your score. Some exams may penalize you for wrong answers, so in such cases *only*, you may not want to guess unless you have some basis for your answer.

7) Suggestions
   a. Objective-type questions
      1. Examine the question booklet for proper sequence of pages and questions
      2. Read all instructions carefully
      3. Skip any question which seems too difficult; return to it after all other questions have been answered
      4. Apportion your time properly; do not spend too much time on any single question or group of questions
      5. Note and underline key words – *all, most, fewest, least, best, worst, same, opposite*, etc.
      6. Pay particular attention to negatives
      7. Note unusual option, e.g., unduly long, short, complex, different or similar in content to the body of the question
      8. Observe the use of "hedging" words – *probably, may, most likely*, etc.
      9. Make sure that your answer is put next to the same number as the question
      10. Do not second-guess unless you have good reason to believe the second answer is definitely more correct
      11. Cross out original answer if you decide another answer is more accurate; do not erase until you are ready to hand your paper in
      12. Answer all questions; guess unless instructed otherwise
      13. Leave time for review

   b. Essay questions
      1. Read each question carefully
      2. Determine exactly what is wanted. Underline key words or phrases.
      3. Decide on outline or paragraph answer

4. Include many different points and elements unless asked to develop any one or two points or elements
5. Show impartiality by giving pros and cons unless directed to select one side only
6. Make and write down any assumptions you find necessary to answer the questions
7. Watch your English, grammar, punctuation and choice of words
8. Time your answers; don't crowd material

8) Answering the essay question

Most essay questions can be answered by framing the specific response around several key words or ideas. Here are a few such key words or ideas:

M's: manpower, materials, methods, money, management
P's: purpose, program, policy, plan, procedure, practice, problems, pitfalls, personnel, public relations
   a. Six basic steps in handling problems:
      1. Preliminary plan and background development
      2. Collect information, data and facts
      3. Analyze and interpret information, data and facts
      4. Analyze and develop solutions as well as make recommendations
      5. Prepare report and sell recommendations
      6. Install recommendations and follow up effectiveness

   b. Pitfalls to avoid
      1. *Taking things for granted* – A statement of the situation does not necessarily imply that each of the elements is necessarily true; for example, a complaint may be invalid and biased so that all that can be taken for granted is that a complaint has been registered
      2. *Considering only one side of a situation* – Wherever possible, indicate several alternatives and then point out the reasons you selected the best one
      3. *Failing to indicate follow up* – Whenever your answer indicates action on your part, make certain that you will take proper follow-up action to see how successful your recommendations, procedures or actions turn out to be
      4. *Taking too long in answering any single question* – Remember to time your answers properly

IX. AFTER THE TEST

Scoring procedures differ in detail among civil service jurisdictions although the general principles are the same. Whether the papers are hand-scored or graded by machine we have described, they are nearly always graded by number. That is, the person who marks the paper knows only the number – never the name – of the applicant. Not until all the papers have been graded will they be matched with names. If other tests, such as training and experience or oral interview ratings have been given, scores will be combined. Different parts of the examination usually have different weights. For example, the written test might count 60 percent of the final grade, and a rating of training and experience 40 percent. In many jurisdictions, veterans will have a certain number of points added to their grades.

After the final grade has been determined, the names are placed in grade order and an eligible list is established. There are various methods for resolving ties between those who get the same final grade – probably the most common is to place first the name of the person whose application was received first. Job offers are made from the eligible list in the order the names appear on it. You will be notified of your grade and your rank as soon as all these computations have been made. This will be done as rapidly as possible.

People who are found to meet the requirements in the announcement are called "eligibles." Their names are put on a list of eligible candidates. An eligible's chances of getting a job depend on how high he stands on this list and how fast agencies are filling jobs from the list.

When a job is to be filled from a list of eligibles, the agency asks for the names of people on the list of eligibles for that job. When the civil service commission receives this request, it sends to the agency the names of the three people highest on this list. Or, if the job to be filled has specialized requirements, the office sends the agency the names of the top three persons who meet these requirements from the general list.

The appointing officer makes a choice from among the three people whose names were sent to him. If the selected person accepts the appointment, the names of the others are put back on the list to be considered for future openings.

That is the rule in hiring from all kinds of eligible lists, whether they are for typist, carpenter, chemist, or something else. For every vacancy, the appointing officer has his choice of any one of the top three eligibles on the list. This explains why the person whose name is on top of the list sometimes does not get an appointment when some of the persons lower on the list do. If the appointing officer chooses the second or third eligible, the No. 1 eligible does not get a job at once, but stays on the list until he is appointed or the list is terminated.

X. HOW TO PASS THE INTERVIEW TEST

The examination for which you applied requires an oral interview test. You have already taken the written test and you are now being called for the interview test – the final part of the formal examination.

You may think that it is not possible to prepare for an interview test and that there are no procedures to follow during an interview. Our purpose is to point out some things you can do in advance that will help you and some good rules to follow and pitfalls to avoid while you are being interviewed.

What is an interview supposed to test?

The written examination is designed to test the technical knowledge and competence of the candidate; the oral is designed to evaluate intangible qualities, not readily measured otherwise, and to establish a list showing the relative fitness of each candidate – as measured against his competitors – for the position sought. Scoring is not on the basis of "right" and "wrong," but on a sliding scale of values ranging from "not passable" to "outstanding." As a matter of fact, it is possible to achieve a relatively low score without a single "incorrect" answer because of evident weakness in the qualities being measured.

Occasionally, an examination may consist entirely of an oral test – either an individual or a group oral. In such cases, information is sought concerning the technical knowledges and abilities of the candidate, since there has been no written examination for this purpose. More commonly, however, an oral test is used to supplement a written examination.

Who conducts interviews?

The composition of oral boards varies among different jurisdictions. In nearly all, a representative of the personnel department serves as chairman. One of the members of the board may be a representative of the department in which the candidate would work. In some cases, "outside experts" are used, and, frequently, a businessman or some other representative of the general public is asked to serve. Labor and management or other special groups may be represented. The aim is to secure the services of experts in the appropriate field.

However the board is composed, it is a good idea (and not at all improper or unethical) to ascertain in advance of the interview who the members are and what groups they represent. When you are introduced to them, you will have some idea of their backgrounds and interests, and at least you will not stutter and stammer over their names.

What should be done before the interview?

While knowledge about the board members is useful and takes some of the surprise element out of the interview, there is other preparation which is more substantive. It *is* possible to prepare for an oral interview – in several ways:

1) Keep a copy of your application and review it carefully before the interview

This may be the only document before the oral board, and the starting point of the interview. Know what education and experience you have listed there, and the sequence and dates of all of it. Sometimes the board will ask you to review the highlights of your experience for them; you should not have to hem and haw doing it.

2) Study the class specification and the examination announcement

Usually, the oral board has one or both of these to guide them. The qualities, characteristics or knowledges required by the position sought are stated in these documents. They offer valuable clues as to the nature of the oral interview. For example, if the job involves supervisory responsibilities, the announcement will usually indicate that knowledge of modern supervisory methods and the qualifications of the candidate as a supervisor will be tested. If so, you can expect such questions, frequently in the form of a hypothetical situation which you are expected to solve. NEVER go into an oral without knowledge of the duties and responsibilities of the job you seek.

3) Think through each qualification required

Try to visualize the kind of questions you would ask if you were a board member. How well could you answer them? Try especially to appraise your own knowledge and background in each area, *measured against the job sought*, and identify any areas in which you are weak. Be critical and realistic – do not flatter yourself.

4) Do some general reading in areas in which you feel you may be weak

For example, if the job involves supervision and your past experience has NOT, some general reading in supervisory methods and practices, particularly in the field of human relations, might be useful. Do NOT study agency procedures or detailed manuals. The oral board will be testing your understanding and capacity, not your memory.

5) Get a good night's sleep and watch your general health and mental attitude

You will want a clear head at the interview. Take care of a cold or any other minor ailment, and of course, no hangovers.

What should be done on the day of the interview?

Now comes the day of the interview itself. Give yourself plenty of time to get there. Plan to arrive somewhat ahead of the scheduled time, particularly if your appointment is in the fore part of the day. If a previous candidate fails to appear, the board might be ready for you a bit early. By early afternoon an oral board is almost invariably behind schedule if there are many candidates, and you may have to wait. Take along a book or magazine to read, or your application to review, but leave any extraneous material in the waiting room when you go in for your interview. In any event, relax and compose yourself.

The matter of dress is important. The board is forming impressions about you – from your experience, your manners, your attitude, and your appearance. Give your personal appearance careful attention. Dress your best, but not your flashiest. Choose conservative, appropriate clothing, and be sure it is immaculate. This is a business interview, and your appearance should indicate that you regard it as such. Besides, being well groomed and properly dressed will help boost your confidence.

Sooner or later, someone will call your name and escort you into the interview room. *This is it.* From here on you are on your own. It is too late for any more preparation. But remember, you asked for this opportunity to prove your fitness, and you are here because your request was granted.

What happens when you go in?

The usual sequence of events will be as follows: The clerk (who is often the board stenographer) will introduce you to the chairman of the oral board, who will introduce you to the other members of the board. Acknowledge the introductions before you sit down. Do not be surprised if you find a microphone facing you or a stenotypist sitting by. Oral interviews are usually recorded in the event of an appeal or other review.

Usually the chairman of the board will open the interview by reviewing the highlights of your education and work experience from your application – primarily for the benefit of the other members of the board, as well as to get the material into the record. Do not interrupt or comment unless there is an error or significant misinterpretation; if that is the case, do not hesitate. But do not quibble about insignificant matters. Also, he will usually ask you some question about your education, experience or your present job – partly to get you to start talking and to establish the interviewing "rapport." He may start the actual questioning, or turn it over to one of the other members. Frequently, each member undertakes the questioning on a particular area, one in which he is perhaps most competent, so you can expect each member to participate in the examination. Because time is limited, you may also expect some rather abrupt switches in the direction the questioning takes, so do not be upset by it. Normally, a board member will not pursue a single line of questioning unless he discovers a particular strength or weakness.

After each member has participated, the chairman will usually ask whether any member has any further questions, then will ask you if you have anything you wish to add. Unless you are expecting this question, it may floor you. Worse, it may start you off on an extended, extemporaneous speech. The board is not usually seeking more information. The question is principally to offer you a last opportunity to present further qualifications or to indicate that you have nothing to add. So, if you feel that a significant qualification or characteristic has been overlooked, it is proper to point it out in a sentence or so. Do not compliment the board on the thoroughness of their examination – they have been sketchy, and you know it. If you wish, merely say, "No thank you, I have nothing further to add." This is a point where you can "talk yourself out" of a good impression or fail to present an important bit of information. Remember, *you close the interview yourself.*

The chairman will then say, "That is all, Mr. _____, thank you." Do not be startled; the interview is over, and quicker than you think. Thank him, gather your belongings and take your leave. Save your sigh of relief for the other side of the door.

How to put your best foot forward

Throughout this entire process, you may feel that the board individually and collectively is trying to pierce your defenses, seek out your hidden weaknesses and embarrass and confuse you. Actually, this is not true. They are obliged to make an appraisal of your qualifications for the job you are seeking, and they want to see you in your best light. Remember, they must interview all candidates and a non-cooperative candidate may become a failure in spite of their best efforts to bring out his qualifications. Here are 15 suggestions that will help you:

1) Be natural – Keep your attitude confident, not cocky

If you are not confident that you can do the job, do not expect the board to be. Do not apologize for your weaknesses, try to bring out your strong points. The board is interested in a positive, not negative, presentation. Cockiness will antagonize any board member and make him wonder if you are covering up a weakness by a false show of strength.

2) Get comfortable, but don't lounge or sprawl

Sit erectly but not stiffly. A careless posture may lead the board to conclude that you are careless in other things, or at least that you are not impressed by the importance of the occasion. Either conclusion is natural, even if incorrect. Do not fuss with your clothing, a pencil or an ashtray. Your hands may occasionally be useful to emphasize a point; do not let them become a point of distraction.

3) Do not wisecrack or make small talk

This is a serious situation, and your attitude should show that you consider it as such. Further, the time of the board is limited – they do not want to waste it, and neither should you.

4) Do not exaggerate your experience or abilities

In the first place, from information in the application or other interviews and sources, the board may know more about you than you think. Secondly, you probably will not get away with it. An experienced board is rather adept at spotting such a situation, so do not take the chance.

5) If you know a board member, do not make a point of it, yet do not hide it

Certainly you are not fooling him, and probably not the other members of the board. Do not try to take advantage of your acquaintanceship – it will probably do you little good.

6) Do not dominate the interview

Let the board do that. They will give you the clues – do not assume that you have to do all the talking. Realize that the board has a number of questions to ask you, and do not try to take up all the interview time by showing off your extensive knowledge of the answer to the first one.

7) Be attentive

You only have 20 minutes or so, and you should keep your attention at its sharpest throughout. When a member is addressing a problem or question to you, give him your undivided attention. Address your reply principally to him, but do not exclude the other board members.

8) Do not interrupt

A board member may be stating a problem for you to analyze. He will ask you a question when the time comes. Let him state the problem, and wait for the question.

9) Make sure you understand the question

Do not try to answer until you are sure what the question is. If it is not clear, restate it in your own words or ask the board member to clarify it for you. However, do not haggle about minor elements.

10) Reply promptly but not hastily

A common entry on oral board rating sheets is "candidate responded readily," or "candidate hesitated in replies." Respond as promptly and quickly as you can, but do not jump to a hasty, ill-considered answer.

11) Do not be peremptory in your answers

A brief answer is proper – but do not fire your answer back. That is a losing game from your point of view. The board member can probably ask questions much faster than you can answer them.

12) Do not try to create the answer you think the board member wants

He is interested in what kind of mind you have and how it works – not in playing games. Furthermore, he can usually spot this practice and will actually grade you down on it.

13) Do not switch sides in your reply merely to agree with a board member

Frequently, a member will take a contrary position merely to draw you out and to see if you are willing and able to defend your point of view. Do not start a debate, yet do not surrender a good position. If a position is worth taking, it is worth defending.

14) Do not be afraid to admit an error in judgment if you are shown to be wrong

The board knows that you are forced to reply without any opportunity for careful consideration. Your answer may be demonstrably wrong. If so, admit it and get on with the interview.

15) Do not dwell at length on your present job

The opening question may relate to your present assignment. Answer the question but do not go into an extended discussion. You are being examined for a *new* job, not your present one. As a matter of fact, try to phrase ALL your answers in terms of the job for which you are being examined.

Basis of Rating

Probably you will forget most of these "do's" and "don'ts" when you walk into the oral interview room. Even remembering them all will not ensure you a passing grade. Perhaps you did not have the qualifications in the first place. But remembering them will help you to put your best foot forward, without treading on the toes of the board members.

Rumor and popular opinion to the contrary notwithstanding, an oral board wants you to make the best appearance possible. They know you are under pressure – but they also want to see how you respond to it as a guide to what your reaction would be under the pressures of the job you seek. They will be influenced by the degree of poise you display, the personal traits you show and the manner in which you respond.

ABOUT THIS BOOK

This book contains tests divided into Examination Sections. Go through each test, answering every question in the margin. At the end of each test look at the answer key and check your answers. On the ones you got wrong, look at the right answer choice and learn. Do not fill in the answers first. Do not memorize the questions and answers, but understand the answer and principles involved. On your test, the questions will likely be different from the samples. Questions are changed and new ones added. If you understand these past questions you should have success with any changes that arise. Tests may consist of several types of questions. We have additional books on each subject should more study be advisable or necessary for you. Finally, the more you study, the better prepared you will be. This book is intended to be the last thing you study before you walk into the examination room. Prior study of relevant texts is also recommended. NLC publishes some of these in our Fundamental Series. Knowledge and good sense are important factors in passing your exam. Good luck also helps. So now study this Passbook, absorb the material contained within and take that knowledge into the examination. Then do your best to pass that exam.

———

EXAMINATION SECTION

EXAMINATION SECTION
TEST 1

<u>Memory for Addresses Test</u>

DIRECTIONS: In this test you will have to memorize the locations (A, B, C, D or E) of 25 addresses shown in five boxes. For example, "Sardis" is in box "C," "4300-4799 West" is in box "E," etc. Study the locations of the addresses for five minutes (try sounding them to yourself), then cover the boxes and try to answer the questions below. *PRINT THE LETTER OF THE CORRECT ANSWER IN THE SPACE AT THE RIGHT.*

Box A	Box B	Box C
4700-5599 Table	6800-6999 Table	5600-6499 Table
Lismore	Kelford	Joel
4800-5199 West	5200-5799 West	3200-3499 West
Hesper	Musella	Sardis
5500-6399 Blake	4800-5499 Blake	6400-7299 Blake

BoxD	BoxE
6500-6799 Table	4400-4699 Table
Tatum	Ruskin
3500-4299 West	4300-4799 West
Porter	Somers
4300-4799 Blake	7300-7499 Blake

1. Musella   1._____

2. 4300-4799 Blake   2._____

3. 4700-5599 Table   3._____

4. Tatum   4._____

5. 5500-6399 Blake   5._____

6. Hesper   6._____

7. Kelford   7._____

8. Somers   8._____

9. 6400-7299 Blake   9._____

10. Joel   10._____

11. 5500-6399 Blake   11._____

12. 5200-5799 West   12._____

13. Porter   13._____

14. 7300-7499 Blake   14._____

KEY (CORRECT ANSWERS)

1.	B	8.	E
2.	D	9.	C
3.	A	10.	C
4.	D	11.	A
5.	A	12.	B
6.	A	13.	D
7.	B	14.	E

———

TEST 2

DIRECTIONS: In this test you will have to decide whether two addresses are alike or different. If the two addresses are exactly alike in every way, mark the answer "A." If the two addresses are different, mark the answer "D." *PRINT THE LETTER OF THE CORRECT ANSWER IN THE SPACE AT THE RIGHT.*

1.	2134 S. 20th St.	2134 S. 20th St.	1.____

1.   2134 S. 20th St.   2134 S. 20th St.   1.____

2.   4608 N. Warnock St.   4806 N. Warnock St.   2.____

3.   1202 W. Girard Dr.   1202 W. Girard Rd.   3.____

4.   Chappaqua, NY 10514   Chappaqua, NY 10514   4.____

5.   2207 Markland Ave.   2207 Markham Ave.   5.____

General Test

DIRECTIONS: In this test there are three kinds of questions Vocabulary, Reading and Number Series. For Vocabulary questions, like number 6, choose the suggested answer that means most nearly the same as the word or words in italics. For Reading questions, like number 7, read the paragraph and answer the question that follows it. For Number Series questions, like numbers 8 through 25, there is a series of numbers which is arranged in some definite order or pattern, followed by five sets of two numbers each. Determine the order or pattern of the numbers at the left and choose from the selections below the two numbers that would properly continue the order or pattern. *PRINT THE LETTER OF THE CORRECT ANSWER IN THE SPACE AT THE RIGHT.*

6.   The reports were *consolidated by* the secretary. *Consolidated* most nearly means   6.____

   A.   combined   B.   concluded   C.   distributed   D.   protected   E.   weighed

7.   "Post office clerks assigned to stamp windows are directly responsible financially in the   7.____
selling of postage. In addition, they are expected to have a thorough knowledge as to the acceptability of matter offered for mailing. Any information which they give out to the public must be accurate."
The paragraph best supports the statement that clerks assigned to stamp-window duty

   A.   must account for stamps issued to them for sale
   B.   have had long training in other post-office work
   C.   advise the public only on matters of official business
   D.   must refer continuously to the sources of postal regulations
   E.   inspect the contents of every package offered for mailing

8.   1 2 3 4 5 6 7 ...   8.____

   A.   1 2   B.   5 6   C.   8 9
   D.   4 5   E.   7 8

9. 15 14 13 12 11 10 9 ...   9.____

    A. 2 1   B. 17 16   C. 8 9
    D. 8 7   E. 9 8

10. 20 20 21 21 22 22 23 ...   10.____

    A. 23 23   B. 23 24   C. 19 19
    D. 22 23   E. 21 22

11. 17 3 17 4 17 5 17 ...   11.____

    A. 6 17   B. 6 7   C. 17 6
    D. 5 6   E. 17 7

12. 1 2 4 5 7 8 10 ...   12.____

    A. 11 12   B. 12 14   C. 10 13
    D. 12 13   E. 11 13

13. 21 21 20 20 19 19 18 ...   13.____

    A. 18 18   B. 18 17   C. 17 18
    D. 17 17   E. 18 19

14. 1 22 1 23 1 24 1 ...   14.____

    A. 26 1   B. 25 26   C. 25 1
    D. 1 26   E. 1 25

15. 1 20 3 19 5 18 7 ...   15.____

    A. 8 9   B. 8 17   C. 17 10
    D. 17 9   E. 9 18

16. 4 7 10 13 16 19 22 ...   16.____

    A. 23 26   B. 25 27   C. 25 26
    D. 25 28   E. 24 27

17. 30 2 28 4 26 6 24 ...   17.____

    A. 23 9   B. 26 8   C. 8 9
    D. 26 22   E. 8 22

18. 5 6 20 7 8 19 9 ...   18.____

    A. 10 18   B. 18 17   C. 10 7
    D. 18 19   E. 10 11

19. 9 10 1 11 12 2 13...   19.____

    A. 2 14   B. 3 14   C. 14 3
    D. 14 15   E. 14 1

20. 4 6 9 11 14 16 19...   20.____

    A. 21 24   B. 22 25   C. 20 22
    D. 21 23   E. 22 24

21. 8 8 1 10 10 3 12 ...   21.____

    A. 13 13   B. 12 5   C. 12 4
    D. 13 5   E. 4 12

22. 14 1 2 15 3 4 16...   22.____

    A. 5 16   B. 6 7   C. 5 17
    D. 5 6   E. 17 5

23. 10 12 50 15 17 50 20 ...   23.____

    A. 50 21   B. 21 50   C. 50 22
    D. 22 50   E. 22 24

24. 1 2 3 50 4 5 6 51 7 8...   24.____

    A. 9 10   B. 9 52   C. 51 10
    D. 10 52   E. 10 50

25. 20 21 23 24 27 28 32 33 38 39 ...   25.____

    A. 45 46   B. 45 52   C. 44 45
    D. 44 49   E. 40 46

KEY (CORRECT ANSWERS)

1.	A		11.	A
2.	D		12.	E
3.	D		13.	B
4.	A		14.	C
5.	D		15.	D
6.	A		16.	D
7.	A		17.	E
8.	C		18.	A
9.	D		19.	C
10.	B		20.	A

21. B
22. D
23. D
24. B
25. A

WORD MEANING

SAMPLE QUESTIONS

In both the Clerk-Carrier and Mail Handler examinations, you will have questions about the meaning of words, or vocabulary. There is a word-meaning part in the Mail Handler examination and a word-meaning section in the Clerk-Carrier examination. The words used in the test for Mail Handler are easier than the ones for Clerk-Carrier.

In this kind of question you have to say what a word or phrase means. (A phrase is a group of words.) This word or phrase is in *italics* in a sentence. You are also given for each question five other words or groups of words---lettered A, B, C, D, and E----as possible answers. One of these words or groups of words means the same as the word or group of words in italics. Only one is right. You are to pick out the one that is right and darken the box that has the letter of your answer.

Hints for Answering Word-Meaning Questions
- Read each question carefully.
- Choose the best answer of the five choices even though it is not the word you might use yourself
- Answer first those that you know. Then do the others.
- If you know that some of the suggested answers are not right, pay no more attention to them.
- Be sure that you have marked an answer for every question, even if you have to guess.

Now study the sample questions and explanations before going on to the Practice Tests.
Word Meaning-Sample Questions
Now try a few.
The letter was *short*. Short means most nearly

A.	tall	D.	heavy
B.	wide	E.	dark
C.	brief		

Short is a word you have used to describe something that is small, or not long, or little, etc. There fore you would not have to spend much time figuring out the right answer. You would choose c) brief

Try another.
The young man is *vigorous*. *Vigorous* means most nearly

A.	serious	D.	strong
B.	reliable	E.	talented
C.	courageous		

Vigorous is a word that you have probably used yourself or read somewhere. It carries with it the idea of being active, full of pep, etc. Which one of the five choices comes closest to meaning that? Certainly not A) serious, B) reliable or E) talented; C) courageous-maybe, D) strong-maybe. But between courageous or strong, you would have to agree that strong is the better choice. Therefore you would choose D.

TEST 1

Now that you know what to do, try these. These words are like those in the Mail Handler examination.

For each question, darken the box for the correct answer. Mark your answers on the answer sheet on the next page.

Answer first those questions for which you know the answers. Then work on the other questions. If you can't figure out the answer, guess.

Do not spend more than 30 minutes on this practice test.

1. *Simple* clothing should be worn to work. *Simple* means most nearly

   A. plain
   B. inexpensive
   C. nice
   D. comfortable
   E. old

2. Take your *finished* work to that area of the work floor. *Finished* means most nearly

   A. inspected
   B. assigned
   C. outgoing
   D. completed
   E. rejected

3. If we are not careful, the problem will *develop* further. *Develop* means most nearly

   A. continue
   B. appear
   C. be used
   D. grow
   E. be concerned

4. The mail handler was a *rapid* worker. *Rapid* means most nearly

   A. trained
   B. rash
   C. fast
   D. regular
   E. strong

5. The supply of envelopes is *abundant* for our use. *Abundant* means most nearly

   A. accessible
   B. plentiful
   C. concentrated
   D. divided
   E. scattered

6. The department is working on *experiments* in that area. *Experiments* means most nearly

   A. tests
   B. refinements
   C. statements
   D. plans
   E. patents

7. The members were concerned about two *fundamental* points. *Fundamental* means most nearly

   A. difficult
   B. serious
   C. emphasized
   D. essential
   E. final

8. The leader *asserted* that it was time to start. *Asserted* means most nearly

   A. believed
   B. decided
   C. declared
   D. agreed
   E. contradicted

9. All requests for supplies should be stated *exactly*. *Exactly* means most nearly

    A. briefly   D. emphatically
    B. clearly   E. accurately
    C. promptly

10. We had not meant to *alarm* them. *Alarm* means most nearly

    A. endanger   D. frighten
    B. insult   E. confuse
    C. accuse

11. The kind of car he bought was *costly*. *Costly* means most nearly

    A. custom made   D. cheap
    B. expensive   E. scarce
    C. desirable

12. The cause of the action was *revealed* before the meeting. *Revealed* means most nearly

    A. made known
    B. fully described
    C. carefully hidden
    D. guessed at
    E. seriously questioned

13. The material used to make mail sacks is *durable*. *Durable* means most nearly

    A. thick   D. elastic
    B. waterproof   E. light
    C. lasting

14. The *valiant* men and women were rewarded. *Valiant* means most nearly

    A. brave   D. loyal
    B. popular   E. famous
    C. victorious

15. The worker was affected by his *fatigue*. *Fatigue* means most nearly

    A. problem   D. u) sickness
    B. weariness   E. worry
    C. relaxation

16. The meeting was interrupted by an *urgent* call. *Urgent* means most nearly

    A. trivial   D. surprising
    B. annoying   E. casual
    C. pressing

17. The captain of the team will *participate in* the ceremony. *Participate in* means most nearly

    A. depend upon   D. supervise
    B. be recognized at   E. share in
    C. be invited to

18. Each office was asked to *restrict* the number of forms it used. *Restrict* means most nearly

    A. watch   D. replace
    B. record   E. provide
    C. limit

19. The pole was *rigid*. *Rigid* means most nearly

    A. broken   D. rough
    B. pointed   E. stiff
    C. bent

20. The supervisor *demonstrated* the sorting procedure. *Demonstrated* means most nearly

    A. changed   D. showed
    B. controlled   E. described
    C. determined

21. The effort was *futile*. *Futile* means most nearly

    A. wasteful   D. undesirable
    B. useless   E. unfortunate
    C. foolish

22. There was a pile of *sundry* items on the table. *Sundry* means most nearly

    A. miscellaneous   D. necessary
    B. valuable   E. specific
    C. unusual

23. The supervisor should not be *partial*. *Partial* means most nearly

    A. biased   D. jealous
    B. greedy   E. suspicious
    C. irresponsible

24. The retired postal worker led an *inactive* life. *Inactive* means most nearly

    A. restful   D. ordinary
    B. idle   E. weary
    C. peaceful

SAMPLE ANSWER SHEET

PART C

1 2 3 4 5 6 7 8
9 10 11 12 13 14 15 16
17 18 19 20 21 22 23 24

Now check your answers by comparing them with the correct answers shown below.

CORRECT ANSWER

PART C

1 2 3 4 5 6 7 8
9 10 11 12 13 14 15 16
17 18 19 20 21 22 23 24

Count, how many you got right, and write that number on this line _____ _____
(This is your Test Score.)

Meaning of Test Score

If your Test Score is *18 or over,* you have a Good score.
If your Test Score is from *15 to 17, you* have a Fair score.
If your Test Score is *14 or less,* you are not doing too well.

TEST 2

This practice test is a little harder.

For each question, darken the box for the correct answer. Mark your answers on the answer sheet on the next page.

Answer first those questions for which you know the answers. Then work on the other questions. If you can't figure out the answer, guess.

Do not spend more than *30 minutes* on this practice test.

1. The officials *prevented* the action. *Prevented* means most nearly

    A. allowed
    B. urged
    C. hindered

    D. considered
    E. suggested

2. The postmaster's office expected to *report* the results next week. *Report* means most nearly

    A. decide
    B. tell
    C. approve

    D. study
    E. repeat

3. The conference room is now *vacant*. *Vacant* means most nearly

    A. empty
    B. quiet
    C. dark

    D. available
    E. lonely

4. Tapping on the desk can be an *irritating* habit. *Irritating* means most nearly

    A. nervous
    B. annoying
    C. noisy

    D. startling
    E. unsuitable

5. The package was *forwarded* by our office. *Forwarded* means most nearly

    A. returned
    B. canceled
    C. received

    D. detained
    E. sent

6. The postal service is *essential* in this country. *Essential* means most nearly

    A. inevitable
    B. needless
    C. economical

    D. indispensable
    E. established

7. The wheel turned at a *uniform* rate. *Uniform* means most nearly

    A. increasing
    B. unusual
    C. normal

    D. slow
    E. unchanging

8. Each carrier realized his *obligation. Obligation* means most nearly

   A. importance
   B. need
   C. duty

   D. n) kindness
   E. honor

9. The group was interested in the *origin* of the rumor. *Origin* means most nearly

   A. direction
   B. growth
   C. existence

   D. beginning
   E. end

10. Laws governing the *parole* of prisoners should be more flexible. *Parole* means most nearly

    A. conditional release
    B. withdrawal of privileges
    C. good behavior
    D. outside employment
    E. solitary confinement

11. That employee is *retiring* by nature. *Retiring* means most nearly

    A. complaining
    B. gruff
    C. neglected

    D. modest
    E. sluggish

12. The patron verified the contents of the package. *Verified* means most nearly

    A. justified
    B. explained
    C. confirmed

    D. guaranteed
    E. examined

13. The group was *repulsed* immediately. *Repulsed* means most nearly

    A. rebuffed
    B. excused
    C. mistreated

    D. loathed
    E. resented

14. The time was right for the committee to make a *decisive* statement. *Decisive* means most nearly

    A. official
    B. prompt
    C. judicial

    D. rational
    E. conclusive

15. Each person expects *compensation* for his work. *Compensation* means most nearly

    A. fulfillment
    B. remuneration
    C. appreciation

    D. approval
    E. recommendation

16. The department plans to increase the number of *novices* in the program. *Novices* means most nearly

    A. volunteers
    B. experts
    C. trainers

    D. beginners
    E. amateurs

17. The guests were overwhelmed by *the fabulous* decorations. *Fabulous* means most nearly

    A. antiquated
    B. enormous
    C. incredible
    D. immoderate
    E. intricate

18. The duties of the job are mentioned *explicitly* in the handbook. *Explicitly* means most nearly

    A. casually
    B. informally
    C. intelligibly
    D. exclusively
    E. specifically

19. The school is supplying opportunities for *recreation*. *Recreation* means most nearly

    A. diversion
    B. eating
    C. resting
    D. learning
    E. recess

20. It was necessary to *recapitulate* the regulation. *Recapitulate* means most nearly

    A. emphasize
    B. withdraw
    C. reinstate
    D. interpret
    E. summarize

21. The villagers *succumbed to* the enemy forces. *Succumbed to* means most nearly

    A. aided
    B. opposed
    C. yielded to
    D. were checked by
    E. discouraged

22. The shipments have been *accelerated*. *Accelerated* means most nearly

    A. anxiously awaited
    B. caused to move faster
    C. delayed by traffic congestion
    D. given careful handling
    E. routed over shorter lines

23. He was not a good employee, because he was *indolent*. *Indolent* means most nearly

    A. stupid
    B. indifferent
    C. selfish
    D. lazy
    E. incompetent

24. He had been cautioned not to be *vindictive*. *Vindictive* means most nearly

    A. boastful
    B. impolite
    C. impulsive
    D. revengeful
    E. aggressive

SAMPLE ANSWER SHEET

PART C

Now check your answers by comparing them with the correct answers shown below.

CORRECT ANSWER

PART C

Count how many you got right, and write that number on this line _____ _____
(This is your Test Score. The meaning of your Test Score will be found on page 3.)

TEST 3

Here is another practice test.

For each question, darken the box for the correct answer. Mark your answers on the answer sheet on the next page.

Answer first those questions for which yon know the answers. Then work on the other questions. If you can't figure out the answer, guess.

Do not spend more than _30 minutes_ on this practice test.

1. The *power* of that organization cannot be ignored any longer. *Power* means most nearly

   A. size
   B. courage
   C. success
   D. force
   E. ambition

2. The employees reached the *shore* several days later. *Shore* means most nearly

   A. ocean
   B. reef
   C. island
   D. water
   E. coast

3. The *instructor* was enthusiastic. *Instructor* means most nearly

   A. expert
   B. foreman
   C. teacher
   D. beginner
   E. assistant

4. A *responsible* employee is an asset to any business. *Responsible* means most nearly

   A. considerate
   B. trustworthy
   C. smart
   D. experienced
   E. resourceful

5. He was a good clerk because he was *alert*. *Alert* means most nearly

   A. watchful
   B. busy
   C. honest
   D. helpful
   E. faithful

6. The machine was *revolving* rapidly. *Revolving* means most nearly

   A. working
   B. inclining
   C. vibrating
   D. n) turning
   E. producing

7. The canceling machine did not *function* yesterday. *Function* means most nearly

   A. finish
   B. stop
   C. overheat
   D. vibrate
   E. operate

8. The supervisor did not *comprehend* the clerk's excuse. *Comprehend* means most nearly

    A. hear   D. consider
    B. understand   E. accept
    C. suspect

9. His conduct was *becoming*. *Becoming* means most nearly

    A. improved   D. suitable
    B. heroic   E. patient
    C. deliberate

10. The men were not aware of the *hazard*. *Hazard* means most nearly

    A. peril   D. contest
    B. choice   E. damage
    C. decision

11. A *flexible* policy was developed to handle the situation. *Flexible* means most nearly

    A. pliable   D. uniform
    B. weak   E. active
    C. rigid

12. The clerk suggested an *innovation*. *Innovation* means most nearly   12._____

    A. conventional practice
    B. improvement
    C. inadequate change
    D. new method
    E. preliminary trial

13. Many parents *indulge* their children too much. *Indulge* means most nearly

    A. admire   D. coax
    B. humor   E. discipline
    C. flatter

14. The men were *commended* for their actions during the emergency. *Commended* means most nearly

    A. blamed   D. encouraged
    B. reprimanded   E. praised
    C. promoted

15. Two men were *designated* by the postmaster. *Designated* means most nearly

    A. dismissed   D. named
    B. assisted   E. rebuked
    C. instructed

16. The package will be *conveyed* by the employees. *Conveyed* means most nearly

    A. carried   D. refused
    B. wrapped   E. guarded
    C. exchanged

17. It seems *feasible* to start the physical fitness training now. *Feasible* means most nearly

    A. praiseworthy
    B. justifiable
    C. practicable
    D. beneficial
    E. profitable

18. He was a *notorious* rebel. *Notorious* means most nearly

    A. condemned
    B. unpleasant
    C. vexatious
    D. pretentious
    E. well-known

19. The main speaker appeared to be a *pompous* person. *Pompous* means most nearly

    A. narrow-minded
    B. insincere
    C. talkative
    D. self-important
    E. rude

20. The office was surprised that he had *disregarded* his duty. *Disregarded* means most nearly

    A. contemplated
    B. discerned
    C. neglected
    D. resisted
    E. renounced

21. The collector described the *blemish* on the new stamp. *Blemish* means most nearly

    A. color
    B. flaw
    C. design
    D. imprint
    E. figure

22. The *ardor* of the patriot was contagious. *Ardor* means most nearly

    A. anger
    B. desire
    C. zeal
    D. happiness
    E. daring

23. All the employees *vied* for that award. *Vied* means most nearly

    A. contended
    B. cooperated
    C. petitioned
    D. persevered
    E. prepared

24. Immediately after hearing the bad news, the group was in a state of *ferment*. *Ferment* means most nearly

    A. lawlessness
    B. indecision
    C. disintegration
    D. reorganization
    E. agitation

SAMPLE ANSWER SHEET

PART C

	A B C D E		A B C D E		A B C D E		A B C D E		A B C D E		A B C D E		A B C D E		A B C D E
1		2		3		4		5		6		7		8	
9		10		11		12		13		14		15		16	
17		18		19		20		21		22		23		24	

Now check your answers by comparing them with the correct answers shown below.

CORRECT ANSWER

PART C

	A B C D E		A B C D E		A B C D E		A B C D E		A B C D E		A B C D E		A B C D E		A B C D E
1		2		3		4		5		6		7		8	
9		10		11		12		13		14		15		16	
17		18		19		20		21		22		23		24	

Count how many you got right, and write that number on this line _____ _____
(This is your Test Score. The meaning of your Test Score will be found on page 3.)

Number Series

DESCRIPTION OF THE TEST AND SAMPLE QUESTIONS

This test measures your ability to think with numbers instead of words.

In each problem, you are given a series of numbers that are changing according to a rule followed by five sets of 2 numbers each. Your problem is to figure out a rule that would make one of the five sets the next two numbers in the series.

The problems do not use hard arithmetic. The task is merely to see how the numbers are related to each other. The sample questions will explain several types in detail so that you may become familiar with what you have to do.

Hints for Answering Number Series Questions

- Do the ones that are easiest for you first. Then go back and work on the others. Enough time is allowed for you to do all the questions, providing you don't stay too long on the ones you have trouble answering.
- Sound out the series to yourself. You may hear the rule: 2 4 6 8 10 12 14 ... What are the next two numbers?
- Look at the series carefully. You may see the rule: 9 2 9 4 9 6 9 ... What are the next two numbers?
- If you can't hear it or see it, you may have to figure it out by writing down how the numbers are changing: 6 8 16 18 26 28 36 ... What are the next two numbers?
  6^{+2} 8^{+8} 16^{+2} 18^{+8} 26^{+2} 28^{+8} 36 ... What are the next two numbers if this is +2 +8? 36+2=38+8=46 or 38 46. You would mark the letter of the answer that goes with 38 46.
- If none of the answers given fit the rule you have figured out, try again. Try to figure out a rule that makes one of the five answers a correct one.

DON'T SPEND TOO MUCH TIME ON ANY ONE QUESTION. SKIP IT AND COME BACK.
A FRESH LOOK SOMETIMES HELPS.

Number Series - Sample Questions

Let's try a few
Mark your answers for these samples on the Sample Answer Sheet on this page.

1. 1 2 3 4 5 6 7 ....A) 1 2   B) 5 6 c) 8 9 D) 4 5 E)7 8
How are these numbers changing? The numbers in this series are increasing by 1 or the rule is "add 1." If you apply this rule to the series, what would the next two numbers be? 7+1=8+1=9. Therefore, the correct answer is 8 and 9, and you would select c) 8 9 as your answer.

2. 15 14 13 12 11 10 9 .... A) 2 1 B) 17 16 c) 8 9 D) 8 7 E) 9 8
The numbers in this series are decreasing by 1 or the rule is "subtract 1. " If you apply that rule, what would the next two numbers be? 91=81 = 7. The correct answer is 8 and 7, and you would select D) 8 7 as your answer.

```
SAMPLE ANSWER SHEET
  A  B  C  D  E        A  B  C  D  E
1 []  []  []  []  []   2 []  []  []  []  []
  A  B  C  D  E        A  B  C  D  E
3 []  []  []  []  []   4 []  []  []  []  []
  A  B  C  D  E        A  B  C  D  E
5 []  []  []  []  []   6 []  []  []  []  []
  A  B  C  D  E        A  B  C  D  E
7 []  []  []  []  []   8 []  []  []  []  []
  A  B  C  D  E        A  B  C  D  E
9 []  []  []  []  []  10 []  []  []  []  []
```

3. 20 20 21 21 22 22 23........A) 23 23   B) 23 24 c) 19 19   D) 22 23   E) 21 22
In this series each number is repeated and then increased by 1. The rule is "repeat, add 1, repeat, add 1,
etc." The series would be 20^{+0} 20^{+1} 21^{+0} 21^{+1} 22^{+0} 22^{+1} 23^{+0} 23^{+1} 24. The correct answer is 23 and 24, and you should have darkened B on the Sample Answer Sheet for question 3.

4. 17 3 17 4 17 5 17..........A) 6 17   B) 6 7   c) 17 6   D) 5 6   E) 17 7
If you can't find a single rule for all the numbers in a series, see if there are really two series in the problem. This series is the number 17 separated by numbers increasing by 1, starting with 3. If the series were continued for two more numbers, it would read 17 3 17 4 17 5 17 6 17. The correct answer is 6 and 17, and you should have darkened A on the Sample Answer Sheet for question 4.

5. 1 2 4 5 7 8 10..............A) 11 12   B) 12 14 c) 10 13   D) 12 13   E) 11 13
The rule in this series is not easy to see until you actually set down how the numbers are changing: 1^{+1} 2^{+2} 4^{+1} 5^{+2} 7^{+1} 8^{+2} 10. The numbers in this series are increasing first by 1 (that is plus 1) and then by 2 (that is plus 2). If the series were continued for two more numbers, it would read: 1245 7 8 10 (plus 1) which is 11 (plus 2) which is 13. Therefore the correct answer is 11 and 13, and you should have darkened E on the Sample Answer Sheet for question 5.

Now read and work sample questions 6 through 10 and mark your answers on the Sample Answer Sheet on this page.

6.   21 21 20 20 19 19 18 .... A) 18 18   B) 18 17   C) 17 18   D) 17 17   E) 18 19
7.   1 22 1 23 1 24 1 .... A) 2 61   B) 25 26   C) 25 1   D) 1 26   E) 1 25
8.   1 20 3 19 5 18 7 .... A) 8 9   B) 8 17   C) 17 10   D) 17 9   E) 9 18
9.   4 7 10 13 16 19 22 .... A) 23 26   B) 25 27   C) 25 26   D) 25 28   E) 24 27
10. 30 2 28 4 26 6 24 .... A) 23 9   B) 26 8   C) 8 9   D) 26 22   E) 8 22

The correct answers to sample questions 6 to 10 are: 6B, 7c, 8D, 9D, and 10E.

Explanations for questions 6 through 10.

6. Each number in the series repeats itself and then decreases by 1 or minus 1; *21* (repeat) *21* (minus 1) which makes *20* (repeat) *20* (minus 1) which makes *19* (repeat) *19* (minus 1) which makes *18* (repeat) ? (minus 1) ?

7. The number *1* is separated by numbers which begin with *22* and increase by 1; *1 22 1* (increase 22 by 1) which makes *23 1* (increase 23 by 1) which makes *24 1* (increase 24 by 1) which makes ?

8. This is best explained by two alternating seriesone series starts with *1* and increases by 2 or plus 2; the other series starts with *20* and decreases by 1 or minus 1.

$$1\uparrow3\uparrow5\uparrow7\uparrow?$$
$$20\ 19\ 18\ \ ?$$

9. This series of numbers increases by 3 (plus 3) beginning with the first number *4* (plus 3) 7 (plus 3) *10* (plus 3) *13* (plus 3) *16* (plus 3) *19*. (plus 3) *22* (plus 3) ? (plus 3) ?

10. Look for two alternating series-one series starts with *30* and decreases by 2 (minus 2); the other series starts with *2* and increases by 2 (plus 2).

$$30\uparrow28\uparrow26\uparrow24\uparrow?$$
$$2\quad4\quad6\quad?$$

Now try questions 11 to 18. Mark your answers on the Sample Answer Sheet on this page.

11. 5 6 20 7 8 19 9 ....A) 10 18　B) 18 17　C) 10 17　D) 18 19　E) 10 11
12. 9 10 1 11 12 2 13 ....A) 2 14　　B) 3 14　　C) 14 3　　D) 14 15　E) 14 1
13. 4 6 9 11 14 16 19 ....A) 21 24　B) 22 25　C) 20 22　D) 21 23　E) 22 24
14. 8 8 1 10 10 3 12 ....A) 13 13　B) 12 5　　C) 12 4　　D) 13 5　　E) 4 12
15. 14 1 2 15 3 4 16 ....A) 5 16　　B) 6 7　　　C) 5 17　　D) 5 6　　　E) 17 5
16. 10 12 50 15 17 50 20 ....A) 50 21　B) 21 50　C) 50 22　D) 22 50　E) 22 24
17. 1 2 3 50 4 5 6 51 7 8 ....A) 9 10　　B)9 52　　C) 51 10　D) 10 52　E) 10 50
18. 20 21 23 24 27 28 32 33 38 39. ...A) 45 46　B) 45 52　C) 44 45　D) 44 49　E) 40 46

HINTS FOR QUESTIONS 11 THROUGH 18.

11. ALTERNATING SERIES: 5 6↑7 8↑9 ? ↑
　　　　　　　　　　　　　20　19　?

12. ALTERNATING SERIES: 9 10↑11 12↑13 ?↑
　　　　　　　　　　　　　　1　　2　?

13. INCREASES ALTERNATELY BY 2 (PLUS 2)
THEN 3 (PLUS 3) 4 (PLUS 2)
6 (PLUS 3) 9 (PLUS 2) *11* (PLUS 3) *14* (PLUS 2) 1
6 (PLUS 3) *19* (PLUS 2) ? (PLUS 3) ?

14. ALTERNATING SERIES: 8 8↑10 10↑12 ?↑
　　　　　　　　　　　　　　1　　3　?

15. ALTERNATING SERIES: 14↑↑15↑↑16↑ ↑
　　　　　　　　　　　　　12　34　??

16. ALTERNATING SERIES: 10 12↑15 17↑20 ?↑
　　　　　　　　　　　　　50　　50　?

17. ALTERNATING SERIES: 1 2 3↑4 5 6↑7 8 ?↑
　　　　　　　　　　　　　50　　51　?

SAMPLE ANSWER SHEET

	A	B	C	D	E		A	B	C	D	E
11	░	░	░	░	░	12	░	░	░	░	░
13	░	░	░	░	░	14	░	░	░	░	░
15	░	░	░	░	░	16	░	░	░	░	░
17	░	░	░	░	░	18	░	░	░	░	░

18. INCREASES ALTERNATELY BY (PLUS 1), (PLUS 2), (PLUS 1), (PLUS 3), (PLUS 1), (PLUS 4), ETC. -20 (PLUS 1) 21 (PLUS 2) 23 (PLUS 1) 24 (PLUS 3) 27 (PLUS 1) 28 (PLUS 4) 32 (PLUS 1) 33 (PLUS 5) 38 (PLUS 1) 39 (PLUS 6) ? (PLUS 1) ?

THE CORRECT ANSWERS TO THE SAMPLE QUESTIONS ABOVE ARE: 11A, 12C, 13A, 14B, 15D, 16D, 17B, AND 18A.

———

NUMBER SERIES-PRACTICE
TEST 1

DO FIRST THOSE QUESTIONS THAT YOU CAN DO EASILY. THEN GO BACK AND DO THE ONES THAT YOU SKIPPED.

Work *20 minutes* on this test. No more. No less. If you finish before the 20 minutes are up, go over your answers again. Mark your answers on the Answer Sheet on the next page.

1. 10 11 12 10 11 12 10 .... A) 10 11   B) 12 10   C) 11 10   D) 11 12   E) 10 12
2. 4 6 7 4 6 7 4 .... A) 6 7   B) 4 7   C) 7 6   D) 7 4   E) 6 8
3. 7 7 3 7 7 4 7 .... A) 4 5   B) 4 7   C) 5 7   D) 7 5   E) 7 7
4. 3 4 10 5 6 10 7 .... A) 10 8   B) 9 8   C) 8 14   D) 8 9   E) 8 10
5. 6 6 7 7 8 8 9 .... A) 10 11   B) 10 10   C) 9 10   D) 9 9   E) 10 9
6. 3 8 9 4 9 10 5 .... A) 6 10   B) 10 11   C) 9 10   D) 11 6   E) 10 6
7. 2 4 3 6 4 8 5 .... A) 6 10   B) 10 7   C) 10 6   D) 9 6   E) 6 7
8. 11 5 9 7 7 9 5 .... A) 11 3   B) 7 9   C) 7 11   D) 9 7   E) 3 7

9. 12 10 8 8 6 7 4 .... A) 2 2   B) 6 4   C) 6 2   D) 4 6   E) 2 6
10. 20 22 22 19 21 21 18 .... A) 22 22   B) 19 19   C) 20 20   D) 20 17   E) 19 17
11. 5 7 6 10 7 13 8 .... A) 16 9   B) 16 10   C) 9 15   D) 10 15   E) 15 9
12. 13 10 11 15 12 13 17 .... A) 18 14   B) 18 15   C) 15 16   D) 14 15   E) 15 18
13. 30 27 24 21 18 15 12 .... A) 9 3   B) 9 6   C) 6 3   D) 12 9   E) 8 5
14. 3 7 10 5 8 10 7 .... A) 10 11   B) 10 5   C) 10 9   D) 10 10   E) 9 10
15. 12 4 13 6 14 8 15 .... A) 10 17   B) 17 10   C) 10 12   D) 16 10   B) 10 16
16. 21 8 18 20 7 17 19 .... A) 16 18   B) 18 6   C) 6 16   D) 5 15   E) 6 18

17. 14 16 16 18 20 20 22 .... A) 22 24   B) 26 28   C) 24 26   D) 24 24   E) 24 28
18. 5 6 8 9 12 13 17 .... A) 18 23   B) 13 18   C) 18 22   D) 23 24   E) 18 19
19. 1 3 5 5 2 4 6 6 3 .... A) 7 4   B) 5 5   C) 1 3   D) 5 7   E) 7 7
20. 12 24 15 25 18 26 21 .... A) 27 22   B) 24 22   C) 29 24   D) 27 27   E) 27 24
21. 17 15 21 18 10 16 19 .... A) 20 5   B) 5 11   C) 11 11   D) 11 20   E) 15 14
22. 12 16 10 14 8 12 6 .... A) 10 14   B) 10 8   C) 10 4   D) 4 10   E) 4 2
23. 13 4 5 13 6 7 13 .... A) 13 8   B) 8 13   C) 8 9   D) 8 8   E) 7 8
24. 10 10 9 11 11 10 12 .... A) 13 14   B) 12 11   C) 13 13   D) 12 12   E) 12 13

SAMPLE ANSWER SHEET

Now check your answers by comparing them with the correct answers shown below.

CORRECT ANSWER

Count how many you got right, and write that number on this line _____→ _____
(This is your Test Score.)

Meaning of Test Score

If your Test Score is *17 or more,* you have a Good score.
If your Test Score *is from 12 to 16,* you have a Fair score.
If your Test Score is *11 or less,* you are not doing too well.

NUMBER SERIES-PRACTICE
TEST 2

Do first those questions that you can do easily. Then go back and do the ones that you skipped.

Work *20 minutes* on this test. No more. No less. If you finish before the 20 minutes are up, go over your answers again. Mark your answers on the Answer Sheet on the next page.

1. 8 9 9 8 10 10 8 .... A) 11 8   B) 8 13   C) 8 11   D) 11 11   E) 8 8
2. 10 10 11 11 12 12 13 .... A) 15 15   B) 13 13   C) 14 14   D) 13 14   E) 14 15
3. 6 6 10 6 6 12 6 .... A) 6 14   B) 13 6   C) 14 6   D) 6 13   E) 6 6
4. 17 11 5 16 10 4 15 .... A) 13 9   B) 13 11   C) 8 5   D) 9 5   E) 9 3
5. 1 3 2 4 3 5 4 .... A) 6 8   B) 5 6   C) 6 5   D) 3 4   E) 3 5
6. 11 11 10 12 12 11 13 .... A) 12 14   B) 14 12   C) 14 14   D) 13 14   E) 13 12
7. 18 5 6 18 7 8 18 .... A) 9 9   B) 9 10   C) 18 9   D) 8 9   E) 18 7
8. 7 8 9 13 10 11 12 14 13 14... A) 15 16   B) 13 15   C) 14 15   D) 15 15   E) 13 14
   .... A) 15 16   B) 15 17   C) 14 17   D) 15 30   E) 30 17

9. 5 7 30 9 11 30 13 ....
10. 5 7 11 13 17 19 23 .... A) 27 29   B) 25 29   C) 25 27   D) 27 31   E) 29 31
11. 9 15 10 17 12 19 15 21 19 .... A) 23 24   B) 25 23   C) 17 23   D) 23 31   E) 21 24
12. 34 37 30 33 26 29 22 .... A) 17 8   B) 18 11   C) 25 28   D) 25 20   B) 25 18
13. 10 16 12 14 14 12 16 .... A) 14 12   B) 10 18   C) 10 14   D) 14 18   E) 14 16
14. 11 12 18 11 13 19 11 14 .... A) 18 11   B) 16 11   C) 20 11   D) 11 21   E) 17 11
15. 20 9 8 19 10 9 18 11 10 .... A) 19 11   B) 17 10   C) 19 12   D) 17 12   E) 19 10
16. 28 27 26 31 30 29 34 .... A) 36 32   B) 32 31   C) 33 32   D) 33 36   E) 35 36

17. 10 16 14 20 18 24 22 .... A) 28 32   B) 27 26   C) 28 26   D) 26 28   E) 27 28
18. 9 9 7 8 7 7 9 10 5 .... A) 5 11   B) 11 12   C) 5 9   D) 9 11   E) 5 5
19. 5 7 11 17 10 12 16 22 15 17 . A) 27 26   B) 19 23   C) 19 27   D) 21 23   E) 21 27
20. 12 19 13 20 14 21 15 .... A) 16 17   B) 22 16   C) 16 22   D) 15 22   E) 15 16
21. 6 6 8 10 10 12 14 .... A) 14 14   B) 14 16   C) 16 16   D) 12 14   E) 10 10
22. 8 1 9 3 10 5 11 .... A) 7 12   B) 6 12   C) 12 6   D) 7 8   E) 6 7
23. 30 11 24 12 19 14 15 17 12
    21 10 .... A) 23 8   B) 25 8   C) 26 9   D) 24 9   E) 25 9
24. 24 30 29 22 28 27 19 26 25
    15 24 .... A) 14 23   B) 19 18   C) 23 22   D) 25 11   E) 23 10

8

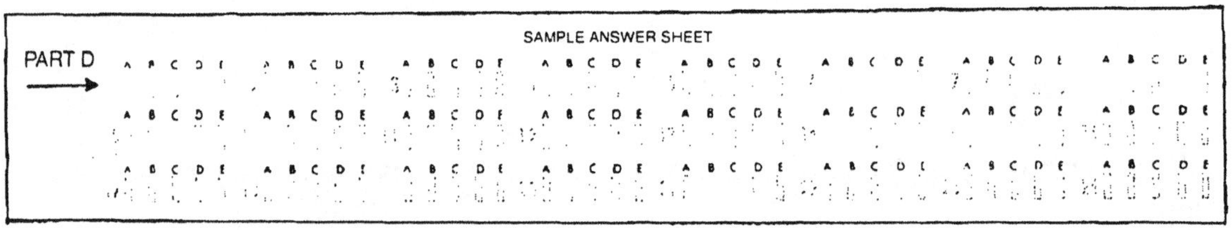
SAMPLE ANSWER SHEET
PART D

Now check your answers by comparing them with the correct answers shown below.

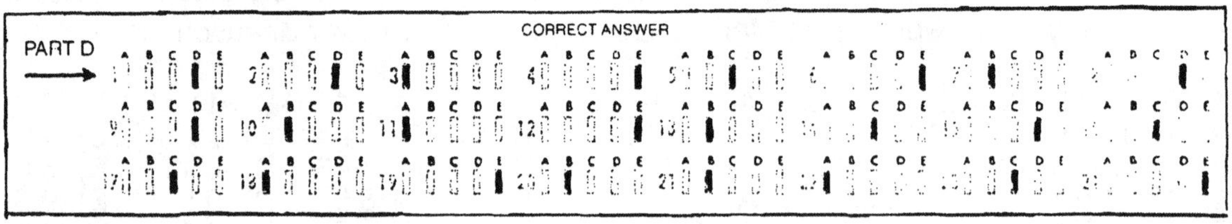
CORRECT ANSWER
PART D

Count how many you got right, and write that number on this line ⟶ ________
(This is your Test Score.)

Meaning of Test Score

If your Test Score is *17 or more,* you have a Good score.
If your Test Score *is from 12 to 16,* you have a Fair score.
If your Test Score is *11 or less,* you are not doing too well.

NUMBER SERIES-PRACTICE
TEST 3

Do first those questions that you can do easily. Then go back and do the ones that you skipped.

Work *20 minutes* on this test. No more. No less. If you finish before the 20 minutes are up, go over your answers again. Mark your answers on the Sample Answer Sheet on the next page.

#	Series	A)	B)	C)	D)	E)
1.	13 12 8 11 10 8 9	8 7	6 8	8 6	8 8	7 8
2.	13 18 13 17 13 16 13	15 13	13 14	13 15	14 15	15 14
3.	13 13 10 12 12 10 11	10 10	10 9	11 9	9 11	11 10
4.	6 5 4 6 5 4 6	4 6	6 4	5 4	5 6	4 5
5.	10 10 9 8 8 7 6	5 5	5 4	6 5	6 4	5 3
6.	20 16 18 14 16 12 14	16 12	10 12	16 18	12 12	12 10
7.	7 12 8 11 9 10 10	11 9	9 8	9 11	10 11	9 10
8.	13 13 12 15 15 14 17	17 16	14 17	16 19	19 19	16 16
9.	19 18 12 17 16 13 15	16 12	14 14	12 14	14 12	12 16
10.	7 15 12 8 16 13 9	17 14	17 10	14 10	14 17	10 14
11.	18 15 6 16 14 6 14	12 6	14 13	6 12	13 12	13 6
12.	6 6 5 8 8 7 10 10	8 12	9 12	12 12	12 9	9 9
13.	17 20 23 26 29 32 35	37 40	41 44	38 41	38 42	36 39
14.	15 5 7 16 9 11 17	18 13	15 17	12 19	13 15	12 13
15.	19 17 16 16 13 15 10	14 7	12 9	14 9	7 12	10 14
16.	11 1 16 10 6 21 9	12 26	26 8	11 26	11 8	8 11
17.	21 21 19 17 17 15 13	11 11	13 11	11 9	9 7	13 13
18.	23 22 20 19 16 15 11	6 5	10 9	6 1	10 6	10 5
19.	17 10 16 9 14 8 11	7 11	7 7	10 4	4 10	7 4
20.	11 9 14 12 17 15 20 18 23	21 24	26 21	21 26	24 27	26 29
21.	7 5 9 7 11 9 13	11 14	10 15	11 15	12 14	10 14
22.	9 10 11 7 8 9 5	6 7	7 8	5 6	6 4	7 5
23.	8 9 10 10 9 10 11 11 10 11 12	11 12	12 10	11 11	12 11	11 13
24.	5 6 8 9 12 13 17 18 23 24	30 31	25 31	29 30	25 30	30 37

SAMPLE ANSWER SHEET

PART D

Now check your answers by comparing them with the correct answers shown below.

CORRECT ANSWER

PART D

Count how many you got right, and write that number on this line ⟶ _____
(This is your Test Score.)

Meaning of Test Score
If your Test Score is *17 or more,* you have a Good score.
If your Test Score *is from 12 to 16,* you have a Fair score.
If your Test Score is *11 or less,* you are not doing too well.

Address Checking

Every member of the Postal work force is responsible for seeing that every letter reaches the right address. If one worker makes an error in reading an address, it can cause a serious delay in getting the letter to where it is supposed to go.

Both the Clerk-Carrier and Mail Handler examinations include tests of address checking. The test in the Clerk-Carrier examination is harder than the one in the Mail Handler examination. The Mail Handler test has only names of cities and states with some zip codes, while the Clerk-Carrier test has street addresses also.

Can you spot whether or not two addresses are alike or different? It is as easy as that. But how fast can you do it accurately? Look at the sample questions below. Each question consists of a pair of addresses like this—

762 W 18th St   762 W 18th St

Are they Alike or Different? They are exactly Alike.

9486 Hillsdale Rd   9489 Hillsdale Rd

Alike or Different? They are Different. Do you see why?

1242 RegalSt   1242 Regel St

Alike or Different?

Remember that this test measures both speed and accuracy. So work as fast as you can without making any mistakes. Have a friend time you while you are working on the practice testsyou may find that you get faster as you become used to this type of question.

Hints for Answering Address-Checking Questions
- Do not spend too much time on any one question.
- The difference may not be noticeable at first, so be sure to check
  —all numbers (are they alike and in the same order or are they different)
  —abbreviations, such as St, Rd, NW, N Y (are they alike or are they different)
  —spellings of street, city, and state names
- Do not get nervous about the time limit. (In the official test no one is expected to do all the questions in the time allowed.)
- Make sure that you have marked the correct box for each question.

Address Checking—Sample Questions

Starting now, if the two addresses are ALIKE darken box A on the Sample Answer Sheet below. If the two addresses are DIFFERENT in any way darken box D. Answer every question.

1 ... 239 Windell Ave   239 Windell Ave
    Alike or Different? Alike. Mark space A for question 1.
2 ... 4667 Edgeworth Rd   4677 Edgeworth Rd
    Alike or Different? Different. Mark space D for question 2.
3 ... 2661 Kennel St SE   2661 Kennel St SW
4 ... 3709 Columbine St   3707 Columbine St
5 ... 969 W 14th St NW   969 W 14th St NW
6 ... 4439 Frederick Pkwy   4439 Frederick Pkwy
7 ... 77 Summers St   77 Summers St
8 ... 828 N Franklin Pl   828 S Franklin Pl

Check your answers with the correct answers. If you have any wrong answers, be sure you see why before you go on.

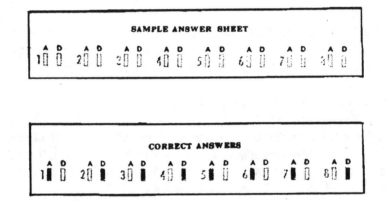

The addresses in the Practice Tests are like the ones you will have to check in the examinations. The ones in Practice Test 1 are like the ones in the Mail Handler examination. Work as fast as you can, but be careful because you will lose points for making mistakes. Be sure to take no more than the correct time for each test. Check your answers with the answers at the end of each test.

Now turn the page and take the first Practice Test.

ADDRESS CHECKING—PRACTICE TEST 1

Work exactly *3 minutes.* No more. No less. If you finish before the 3 minutes are up, go over your answers again. Be sure to mark your answers on the Sample Answer Sheet on the next page.

1 ...	Purdin Mo	Purdon Mo
2 ...	Hobart Ind 46342	Hobart Ind 46342
3 ...	Kuna Idaho	Kuna Idaho
4 ...	Janesville Calif 96114	Janesville Calif 96119
5 ...	Sioux Falls S Dak	Sioux Falls S Dak
6 ...	Homewood Miss	Homewood Miss
7 ...	Kaweah Calif	Kawaeh Calif
8 ...	Unionport Ohio	Unionport Ohio
9 ...	Meyersdale Pa	Meyersdale Va
10 ...	Coquille Oreg 97423	Coqville Oreg 97423
11 ...	Milan Wis	Milam Wis
12 ...	Prospect Ky	Prospect Ky
13 ...	Cloversville N Y	Cloverville N Y
14 ...	Locate Mont 59340	Locate Mont 59340
15 ...	Bozman Md	Bozeman Md
16 ...	Orient Ill	Orient Ill
17 ...	Yosemite Ky 42566	Yosemite Ky 42566
18 ...	Camden Miss 39045	Camden Miss 39054
19 ...	Bennington Vt	Bennington Vt
20 ...	La Farge Wis	La Farge Wis
21 ...	Fairfield N Y	Fairfield N C
22 ...	Wynot Nebr	Wynot Nebr
23 ...	Arona Pa	Aroda Pa
24 ...	Thurman N C 28683	Thurmond N C 28683
25 ...	Zenda Kans	Zenba Kans
26 ...	Pike N H	Pike N H
27 ...	Gorst Wash 98337	Gorst Wash 98837
28 ...	Joiner Ark	Joiner Ark
29 ...	Normangee Tex	Normangee Tex
30 ...	Toccoa Ga	Tococa Ga
31 ...	Small Point Maine 04567	Small Point Maine 04567
32 ...	Eagan Tenn	Eagar Tenn
33 ...	Belfield N Dak	Belford N
34 ...	De Ridder La 70634	Dak De Ridder La 70634
35 ...	Van Meter Iowa	Van Meter Iowa
36 ...	Valparaiso Fla	Valparaiso Ind
37 ...	Souris N Dak	Souris N Dak
38 ...	Robbinston Maine	Robbinstown Maine
39 ...	Dawes W Va 25054	Dawes W Va 25054
40 ...	Goltry Okla	Goltrey Okla

4

PART A

Now check your answers by comparing your answers with the correct answers shown below.

CORRECT ANSWERS

PART A

Count how many you got right, and write that number on this
line————————————————————————► Number Right ————

Now count how many you got wrong, and write that number on
this line————————————————————————► Number Wrong ═══

Subtract the Number Wrong from the Number Right and write
the Difference on this line————————————————► Total Score ————

Meaning of Test Score
　　If your Total Score is *26 or more,* you have a Good score.
　　If your Total Score is from *16 to 25,* you have a Fair score.
　　If your Total Score is *15 or less,* you are not doing too well.
　　　　You may be going too slowly, or you may be making too many mistakes. You need
　　　　more practice.

ADDRESS CHECKING—PRACTICE TEST 2

These addresses are a little harder.

Remember to work as fast as you can but be careful. Work exactly *3 minutes.* No more. No less. If you finish before the 3 minutes are up, go over your answers again. Be sure to mark your answers on the Sample Answer Sheet on the next page.

1 ...	7961 Eastern Ave SE	7961 Eastern Ave SE
2 ...	3809 20th Rd N	3309 20th Rd N
3 ...	Smicksburg Pa	Smithsburg Pa
4 ...	Sherman Conn	Sherman Conn
5 ...	Richland Ga	Richland La
6 ...	8520 Leesburg Pike SE	8520 Leesburg Pike SE
7 ...	Genevia Ark	Geneva Ark
8 ...	104 W Jefferson St	104 W Jefferson St
9 ...	Meandor WVa	Meander W Va
10 ...	6327 W Mari Ct	6327 W Mari Ct
11 ...	3191 Draper Dr SE	3191 Draper Dr SW
12 ...	1415 W Green Spring Rd	1415 W Green Spring Rd
13 ...	Parr Ind	Parr Ind
14 ...	East Falmouth Mass 02536	East Falmouth Miss 02536
15 ...	3016 N St NW	3016 M St NW
16 ...	Yukon Mo	Yukon Mo
17 ...	7057 Brookfield Plaza	7057 Brookfield Plaza
18 ...	Bethel Ohio 45106	Bethel Ohio 45106
19 ...	Littleton N H	Littleton N C
20 ...	8909 Bowie Dr	8909 Bowie Dr
21 ...	Colmar I11	Colmar I11
22 ...	784 Matthews Dr NE	784 Matthews Dr NE
23 ...	2923 John Marshall Dr	2932 John Marshall Dr
24 ...	6023 Woodmont Rd	6023 Woodmount Rd
25 ...	Nolan Tex	Noland Tex
26 ...	342 E Lincolnia Rd	342 E Lincolnia Dr
27 ...	Jane Calif	Jane Calif
28 ...	4921 Seminary Rd	4912 Seminary Rd
29 ...	Ulmers S C	Ullmers S C
30 ...	4804 Montgomery Lane SW	4804 Montgomery Lane SW
31 ...	210 E Fairfax Dr	210 W Fairfax Dr
32 ...	Hanapepe Hawaii	Hanapepe Hawaii
33 ...	450 La Calle del Punto	450 La Calle del Punto
34 ...	Walland Tenn 37886	Walland Tenn 37836
35 ...	Villamont Va	Villamont Va
36 ...	4102 Georgia Ave NW	4102 Georgia Rd NW
37 ...	Aroch Oreg	Aroch Oreg
38 ...	6531 N Walton Ave	6531 N Waldon Ave
39 ...	Jeff Ky	Jeff Ky
40 ...	Delphos Iowa	Delphis Iowa

SAMPLE ANSWER SHEET

PART A → 1 [ ] 2 [ ] 3 [ ] 4 [ ] 5 [ ] 6 [ ] 7 [ ] 8 [ ] 9 [ ] 10 [ ] 11 [ ] 12 [ ] 13 [ ] 14 [ ] 15 [ ]

16 [ ] 17 [ ] 18 [ ] 19 [ ] 20 [ ] 21 [ ] 22 [ ] 23 [ ] 24 [ ] 25 [ ] 26 [ ] 27 [ ] 28 [ ] 29 [ ] 30 [ ] 31 [ ]

32 [ ] 33 [ ] 34 [ ] 35 [ ] 36 [ ] 37 [ ] 38 [ ] 39 [ ] 40 [ ]

Now check your answers by comparing your answers with the correct answers shown below.

CORRECT ANSWERS

PART A → 1 [ ] 2 [ ] 3 [ ] 4 [ ] 5 [ ] 6 [ ] 7 [ ] 8 [ ] 9 [ ] 10 [ ] 11 [ ] 12 [ ] 13 [ ] 14 [ ] 15 [ ]

16 [ ] 17 [ ] 18 [ ] 19 [ ] 20 [ ] 21 [ ] 22 [ ] 23 [ ] 24 [ ] 25 [ ] 26 [ ] 27 [ ] 28 [ ] 29 [ ] 30 [ ] 31 [ ]

32 [ ] 33 [ ] 34 [ ] 35 [ ] 36 [ ] 37 [ ] 38 [ ] 39 [ ] 40 [ ]

Count how many you got right, and write that number on this line ————————————————▶ Number Right ————

Now count how many you got wrong, and write that number on this line ————————————————▶ Number Wrong ————

Subtract the Number Wrong from the Number Right and write the Difference on this line ————————————▶ Total Score ————

Meaning of Test Score

If your Total Score is *26 or more,* you have a Good score.

If your Total Score is from *16 to 25,* you have a Fair score.

If your Total Score is *15 or less,* you are not doing too well.

You may be going too slowly, or you may be making too many mistakes. You need more practice.

ADDRESS CHECKING-PRACTICE TEST 3

These addresses are exactly like the ones in the Clerk-Carrier examination. Even if you don't plan to take the Clerk-Carrier examination, this is good practice for the Mail Handler one. Work as fast as you can without making too many errors. Work exactly *3 minutes*. No more. No less. If you finish before the 3 minutes are up, go over your answers again. Mark your answers on the Sample Answer Sheet on the next page.

1	2134 S 20th St	2134 S 20th St
2	4608 N Warnock St	4806 N Warnock St
3	1202 W Girard Dr	1202 W Girard Rd
4	3120 S Harcourt St	3120 S Harcourt St
5	4618 W Addison St	4618 E Addison St
6	Sessums Miss	Sessoms Miss
7	6425 N Delancey	6425 N Delancey
8	5407 Columbia Rd	5407 Columbia Rd
9	2106 Southern Ave	2106 Southern Ave
10	Highfalls N C 27259	Highlands NC 27259
11	2873 Pershing Dr	2873 Pershing Dr
12	1329 N H Ave NW	1329 N J Ave NW
13	1316 N Quinn St	1316 N Quinn St
14	7507 Wyngate Dr	7505 Wyngate Dr
15	2918 Colesville Rd	2918 Colesvale Rd
16	2071 E Belvedere Dr	2071 E Belvedere Dr
17	Palmer Wash	Palmer Mich
18	2106 16th St SW	2106 16th St SW
19	2207 Markland Ave	2207 Markham Ave
20	5345 16th St SW	5345 16th St SE
21	239 Summit Pl NE	239 Summit Pl NE
22	152 Continental Pkwy	152 Continental Blvd
23	8092 13th Rd S	8029 13th Rd S
24	3906 Queensbury Rd	3906 Queensbury Rd
25	4719 Linnean Ave NW	4719 Linnean Ave NE
26	Bradford Me	Bradley Me
27	Parrott Ga 31777	Parrott Ga 31177
28	4312 Lowell Lane	4312 Lowell Lane
29	6929 W 135th Place	6929 W 135th Plaza
30	5143 Somerset Cir	5143 Somerset Cir
31	8501 Kennedy St	8501 Kennedy St
32	2164 E McLean Ave	2164 E McLean Ave
33	7186 E St NW	7186 F St NW
34	2121 Beechcrest Rd	2121 Beechcroft Rd
35	3609 E Montrose St	3609 E Montrose St
36	324 S Alvadero St	324 S Alverado St
37	2908 Plaza de las Estrellas	2908 Plaza de las Estrellas
38	223 Great Falls Rd SE	223 Great Falls Dr SE
39	Kelton S C 29354	Kelton S C 29354
40	3201 Landover Rd	3201 Landover Rd

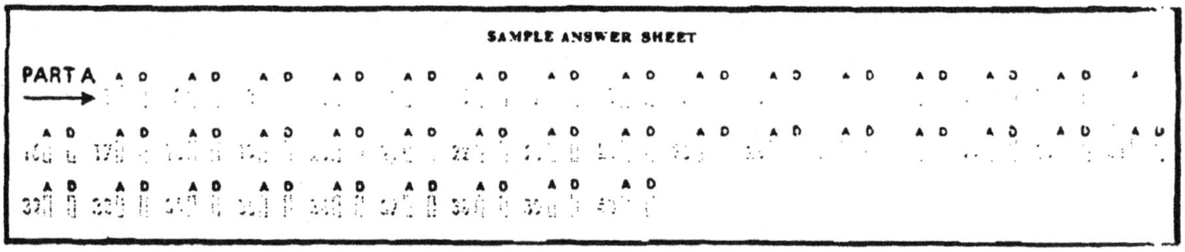
SAMPLE ANSWER SHEET
PART A

Now check your answers by comparing your answers with the correct answers shown below.

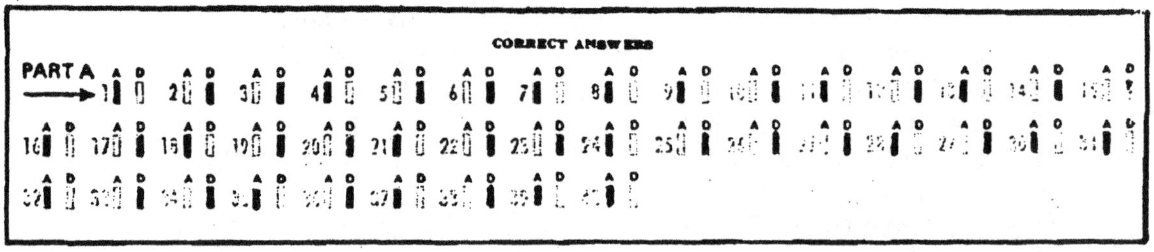
CORRECT ANSWERS
PART A

Count how many you got right, and write that number on this line ⟶ Number Right ________

Now count how many you got wrong, and write that number on this line ⟶ Number Wrong ________

Subtract the Number Wrong from the Number Right and write the Difference on this line ⟶ Total Score ________

Meaning of Test Score.

If your Total Score is *26 or more,* you have a Good score.

If your Total Score is from *16 to 25,* you have a Fair score.

If your Total Score is *15 or less,* you are not doing too well.

You may be going too slowly, or you may be making too many mistakes. You need more practice.

ADDRESS CHECKING
EXAMINATION SECTION
TEST 1

DIRECTIONS: The following test contains 60 questions to be completed in 11 minutes. The two lists below—the correct list on the left and the list to be checked on the right—are to be compared quickly and accurately in that time. Mark your answer A, B, C or D based on the following information:
Mark "A" if the two items are exactly the same (no errors)
Mark "B" if there is an error in the address only
Mark "C" if there is an error in the ZIP code only
Mark "D" if there are errors in both the address and ZIP code
PRINT THE LETTER OF THE CORRECT ANSWER IN THE SPACE AT THE RIGHT.

	CORRECT LIST		LIST TO BE CHECKED		
1.	149 Market St. Purdin, MO	64674	149 Market St. Purdin, MO	64674	1._____
2.	1212 Jeremy Dr. Hobart, IN	46342	1212 Jeremy Dr. Hobart, IN	46432	2._____
3.	39 Union Pkwy. Kuna, ID	83634	39 Union Pkwy. Kuna, ID	83684	3._____
4.	1001 Azalea Blvd. Janesville, CA	96114	1011 Azalea Blvd. Janesville, CA	96119	4._____
5.	991 Rockaway Rd. Sioux Falls, SD	57101	991 Rockaway Rd. Sioux Falls, SD	57101	5._____
6.	75 Gorton St. Homewood, PA	15208	75 Gordon St. Homewood, PA	15208	6._____
7.	154 Kenmore Rd. Kaweah, CA	93237	154 Kenmore Rd. Kawaeh, CA	93237	7._____
8.	501 Flower Rd. Unionport, OH	43910	501 Flower Rd. Unionsport, OH	43910	8._____
9.	198 South Brush Dr. Meyersdale, PA	15552	198 South Brush Dr. Meyersdale, PA	15552	9._____
10.	2109 E. 161st St. Coquille, OR	97423	2109 E. 161st St. Coquille, OR	97432	10._____
11.	331 McDugan Blvd. Milan, WI	54411	331 MacDugan Blvd. Milan, WI	54441	11._____
12.	239 Ellenville St. Prospect, KY	40059	239 Ellenville St. Prospect, NY	40099	12._____

13. 117 Arrow Way Gloversville, NY	12078	117 Arrow Way Gloversville, NY	12078	13._____
14. 226 Bowery Rd. Locate, MT	59340	226 Bowery Rd. Locate, MT	59340	14._____
15. 440 West Shore Dr. Bozman, MD	21612	440 West Shore Dr. Bozeman, MD	21612	15._____
16. 5501 Parker St. Orient, IL	62874	5501 Parker St. Orient, IL	62814	16._____
17. 11 Burke Blvd. Yosemite, KY	42566	11 Burke Blvd. Yosemite, KY	42556	17._____
18. 912 Croxley St. Camden, MS	39045	912 Croxley St. Camden, MS	39045	18._____
19. 54 Maple La. Bennington, VT	05201	54 Maple La. Bennington, VT	05201	19._____
20. 101 Badger Blvd. La Farge, WI	54639	101 Badger Blvd. Le Farge, WI	54633	20._____
21. 201 Westminster Rd. Fairfield, NC	27826	201 Eastminster Rd. Fairfield, NC	27826	21._____
22. 315 Frazier Pl. Wynot, NE	68792	315 Frazier Pl. Wynot, NE	68792	22._____
23. 808 Appleton St. Arona, PA	15617	808 Appleton St. Arona, PA	15677	23._____
24. 2262 Blackberry Dr. Thurmond, NC	28683	2262 Blackberry Dr. Thurmond, NC	28633	24._____
25. 369 Jayhawk Pkwy. Zenda, KS	67159	369 Jayhawk Pkwy. Zenba, KS	67159	25._____
26. 117 Plateau St. Pike, NH	03780	117 Plateau Rd. Pike, NH	03780	26._____
27. 20 Forest Ave. Gorst, WA	98337	20 Forest Ave. Gorst, WA	98337	27._____
28. 400 Littleview Pkwy. Joiner, AR	72350	400 Littleview Pkwy. Joiner, AZ	72530	28._____
29. 211 Fields St. Normangee, TX	77871	211 Fields St. Normangee, TX	77871	29._____

30.	47 Pollack Dr. Toccoa, GA	30577	47 Pollack Dr. Tococa, GA	30057	30._____
31.	4884 Harborport St. Small Point, ME	04567	4884 Harborport St. Small Point, ME	04567	31._____
32.	25 Frank St. Eagan, TN	37730	25 Frank St. Eagar, TN	37330	32._____
33.	38 Lakeview Terr. Belfield, ND	58622	38 Lakeview Terr. Belfield, ND	53622	33._____
34.	1024 Saban St. De Ridder, LA	70634	1024 Saban St. De Ridder, LA	70634	34._____
35.	206 Banks Blvd. Van Meter, IA	50261	206 Banks Blvd. Van Meter, IA	50261	35._____
36.	624 Bryce La. Valparaiso, FL	32580	624 Bryce La. Valparaiso, FL	32580	36._____
37.	11 Hemingway St. Souris, ND	58783	11 Hemmingway St. Souris, ND	58783	37._____
38.	88 Pine St. Robbinston, ME	04671	88 Pine St. Robbinston, ME	04671	38._____
39.	227 Gansey Rd. Dawes, WV	25054	227 Gansey Rd. Dawes, WV	25854	39._____
40.	187 Clayton Ct. Goltry, OK	73739	187 Clayton St. Goltry, OK	73789	40._____
41.	7961 Eastern Ave. SE Jacksonville, FL	32209	7961 Eastern Ave. SE Jacksonville, FL	32209	41._____
42.	3809 20th Rd. Manhattan, KS	66503	3809 20th Rd. Manhattan, NY	66503	42._____
43.	177 Andrews Cir. Smicksburg, PA	16256	177 Andrews Cir. Smicksburg, PA	16266	43._____
44.	90 Birdstone Sq. Sherman, CT	06784	90 Birdstone St. Sherman, CT	06734	44._____
45.	4717 Greene St. Richland, GA	31825	4717 Greene St. Richland, GA	31825	45._____
46.	8520 Leesburg Pike SE Boise, ID	83706	8520 Leesburg Pike SE Boise, ID	83706	46._____

47.	919 Little Bay Pkwy. Genoa, AR	71840	919 Little Bay Pkwy. Genoa, AR	71840	47._____
48.	104 W. Jefferson St. Syracuse, NY	13210	140 W. Jefferson St. Syracuse, NY	13012	48._____
49.	77 Tottenham Pl. Montrose, WV	26283	77 Tottenham Pl. Montross, WV	26283	49._____
50.	6327 W. Mari Ct. San Diego, CA	92129	6237 W. Mari Ct. San Diego, CA	92129	50._____
51.	3191 Draper Dr. Syosset, NY	11791	3191 Draper Dr. Syosset, NY	11771	51._____
52.	1415 Green Spring Rd. Edgewater, FL	32132	1415 Green Spring Rd. Edgewater, FL	32132	52._____
53.	1231 Davis Blvd. Otis, IN	46391	1231 Davis Blvd. Ottis, IN	46991	53._____
54.	820 McMurphy Ave. East Falmouth, MA	02536	820 McMurphy Ave. East Falmouth, MA	02536	54._____
55.	3016 N St. NW Paducah, KY	42001	3016 N St. NW Paducah, KY	42001	55._____
56.	220 Quinn St. Yukon, MO	65589	220 Quinn St. Yukon, MA	65589	56._____
57.	7057 Brookfield Plaza New York, NY	10025	7507 Brookfield Plaza New York, NY	10025	57._____
58.	900 Zwiegert Pl. Bethel, OH	45106	900 Zwiegert Pl. Bethel, OH	45706	58._____
59.	450 Daly Blvd. Littleton, NH	03561	450 Daly Blvd. Littleton, NH	03561	59._____
60.	8909 Bowie Dr. Waukegan, IL	60087	8909 Bowie Dr. Waukegan, IL	60087	60._____

KEY (CORRECT ANSWERS)

1. A	11. D	21. B	31. A	41. A	51. C
2. C	12. D	22. A	32. D	42. B	52. A
3. C	13. A	23. C	33. C	43. C	53. D
4. D	14. A	24. C	34. A	44. D	54. A
5. A	15. B	25. B	35. A	45. A	55. A
6. B	16. C	26. B	36. A	46. A	56. B
7. B	17. C	27. A	37. B	47. A	57. B
8. B	18. A	28. D	38. A	48. D	58. C
9. A	19. A	29. A	39. C	49. B	59. A
10. C	20. D	30. D	40. D	50. B	60. A

TEST 2

DIRECTIONS: The following test contains 60 questions to be completed in 11 minutes. The two lists below—the correct list on the left and the list to be checked on the right—are to be compared quickly and accurately in that time. Mark your answer A, B, C or D based on the following information:

Mark "A" if the two items are exactly the same (no errors)
Mark "B" if there is an error in the address only
Mark "C" if there is an error in the ZIP code only
Mark "D" if there are errors in both the address and ZIP code
PRINT THE LETTER OF THE CORRECT ANSWER IN THE SPACE AT THE RIGHT.

	CORRECT LIST		LIST TO BE CHECKED		
1.	919 Hannigan Blvd. Colmar, IL	62367	919 Hannigan Blvd. Colmar, IL	62367	1._____
2.	784 Matthews Dr. NE Ocala, FL	34476	784 Matthews Dr. Ocala, FL	34776	2._____
3.	2923 John Marshall Dr. Los Angeles, CA	90018	2923 John Marshall Dr. Los Angeles, CA	90008	3._____
4.	6023 Woodmont Rd. Kennesaw, GA	30144	6023 Woodmont Rd. Kennesaw, GA	30144	4._____
5.	127 Wesker Dr. Nolan, TX	79537	127 Wesker Dr. Noland, TX	79537	5._____
6.	342 E. Lincolnia Rd. Leesville, LA	71446	342 E. Lincolnia Rd. Leesville, LA	71446	6._____
7.	201 Montego Dr. Jenner, CA	95450	201 Montego Rd. Jenner, CA	94540	7._____
8.	4921 Seminary Rd. Fairbanks, AK	99709	4921 Seminary Rd. Fairbanks, AK	97709	8._____
9.	310 Felton St. Ulmer, SC	29849	310 Felton St. Ullmer, SC	29349	9._____
10.	4804 Montgomery La. Scottsdale, AZ	85259	4804 Montgomery La. Scottsdale, AZ	85529	10._____
11.	210 E. Fairfax Dr. Athens, GA	30601	210 E. Fairfax Dr. Athens, GA	30601	11._____
12.	450 Pinestraw Rd. Hanapepe, HI	96716	450 Pinestraw Rd. Hanapepe, HI	96716	12._____
13.	450 La Calle del Punto Miami, FL	33174	450 La Calle del Punto Miami, FL	33114	13._____

14. 806 Brennan Ct. Walland, TN	37886	806 Brennan Ct. Walland, TN	37886	14._____
15. 380 Smoken Dr. Villamont, VA	24178	380 Smoken Dr. Villamont, VA	24178	15._____
16. 4102 Georgia Ave. Hollywood, MD	20636	4102 Georgia Ave. Hollywood, MO	20636	16._____
17. 2500 Sisslen St. Arock, OR	97902	2500 Sisslen St. Aroch, OR	97002	17._____
18. 6531 N. Walton Ave. Albany, NY	12222	6531 N. Walton Ave. Albany, NY	12222	18._____
19. 15 Kelly Ave. Jeff, KY	41751	15 Kelly Ave. Jeff, KY	41751	19._____
20. 7240 Avenue K Dyersville, IA	52040	7240 Avenue K Dyersville, IA	52070	20._____
21. 2134 S. 20th St. Tampa, FL	33614	2314 S. 20th St. Tampa, FL	33674	21._____
22. 4608 N. Warnock St. Goshen, IN	46526	4608 N. Warnock St. Gashen, IN	46256	22._____
23. 1202 Girard Dr. Glen Burnie, MD	21061	1202 Girard Dr. Glen Burnie, MD	21061	23._____
24. 3120 S. Harcourt St. Brighton, MI	48116	3120 S. Harcourt St. Brighton, MI	48116	24._____
25. 4618 W. Addison St. Chicago, IL	60613	4618 W. Addison St. Chicago, IL	60613	25._____
26. 909 Eastgate Blvd. Sessums, MS	39759	909 East Gate Blvd. Sessums, MS	39759	26._____
27. 6425 N. Delancey St. St. Paul, MN	55124	6425 N. Delancey St. St. Paul, MN	55124	27._____
28. 5407 Columbia Rd. Billings, MT	59101	5407 Columbia Rd. Billings, MT	59010	28._____
29. 2106 Southern Ave. Glendale, CA	91205	2106 Southern Ave. Glendale, CA	97205	29._____
30. 1045 Chass Ct. Highfalls, NC	27259	1045 Chass Ct. Highfalls, NC	27259	30._____

31.	2873 Pershing Dr. Montgomery, AL	36108	2873 Pershing Dr. Montgomery, AZ	36180	31._____
32.	1329 N.H. Ave. NW Brooklyn, NY	11229	1329 N.H. Ave. NW Brooklyn, NY	11229	32._____
33.	1316 N. Quinn St. Chapel Hill, NC	27514	1316 N. Quin St. Chapel Hill, NC	27514	33._____
34.	7507 Wyngate Dr. Rockville, RI	02873	7507 Wyngate Dr. Rockville, RI	02878	34._____
35.	2918 Colesville Rd. Broomall, PA	19008	2819 Colesville Rd. Broomall, PA	19908	35._____
36.	2071 E. Belvedere Dr. Belton, SC	29627	2071 E. Belvadere Dr. Belton, SC	29927	36._____
37.	400 Sackmon St. Walla Walla, WA	99362	400 Sackmon St. Walla Walla, WA	93962	37._____
38.	2106 16th St. SW Ada, OK	74820	2106 16th St. SW Ada, OK	74820	38._____
39.	2207 Markland Ave. Cleveland, TN	37311	2207 Markland Ave. Cleveland, TN	37311	39._____
40.	5345 Langerhans Dr. Smoot, WY	83126	5345 Langerhans Dr. Smoot, WY	83126	40._____
41.	239 Summit Pl. Odessa, TX	79760	239 Summit Pl. Odessa, TN	79760	41._____
42.	152 Continental Pkwy. Reno, NV	89511	152 Continental Pkwy. Reno, NV	89511	42._____
43.	8092 13th Rd. S Alderson, WV	24910	8092 13th Rd. S Alderson, WV	24810	43._____
44.	3906 Queensbury Rd. Cincinnati, OH	45204	3906 Queensbury Rd. Cincinnati, OH	45004	44._____
45.	4719 Linnean Ave. Dalton, MA	01226	4719 Linnean Ave. Dallton, MA	00226	45._____
46.	5151 Vilma Dr. Bradford, ME	04410	5151 Vilma Dr. Bradford, ME	04410	46._____
47.	153 Abreu Ct. Parrott, GA	31777	153 Abreu St. Parrott, GA	31777	47._____

48. 4312 Lowell La. Bloomfield Hills, MI	48301	4312 Lowell La. Bloomfield Hills, MI	48301	48._____
49. 6929 W. 135th Pl. Rapid City, SD	57709	6929 W. 135th Pl. Rapid City, SD	57509	49._____
50. 5143 Somerset Cir. Montauk, NY	11954	5143 Somerset Cir. Montauk, NY	11994	50._____
51. 8501 Kennedy St. West Chazy, NY	12992	8501 Kennedy St. West Chazy, NY	12992	51._____
52. 2164 E. McLean Ave. Hydro, OK	73048	2164 E. McLean Ave. Hydro, OK	73048	52._____
53. 7186 E St. NW Flint, MI	48501	7186 W St. NE Flint, MI	48051	53._____
54. 2121 Beechcrest Rd. Diamond, OH	44412	2121 Beachcrest Rd. Diamond, OH	44442	54._____
55. 3609 E. Montrose St. Valley Stream, NY	11581	3609 E. Montrose St. Valley Stream, NY	11581	55._____
56. 324 S. Alvadero St. San Antonio, TX	78207	324 S. Alvodero St. San Antonio, TX	78207	56._____
57. 2908 Gordon Rd. Albuquerque, NM	87101	2908 Gordon Rd. Albuquerque, NM	87011	57._____
58. 223 Great Falls Rd. Boston, MA	02101	233 Great Falls Rd. Boston, MA	02101	58._____
59. 201 Highwater Terr. Longs, SC	29568	201 Highwater Terr. Longs, SC	29658	59._____
60. 3201 Landover Rd. Charleston, WV	25328	3201 Landover Rd. Charleston, WV	25328	60._____

KEY (CORRECT ANSWERS)

1. A	11. A	21. D	31. D	41. B	51. A
2. C	12. A	22. D	32. A	42. A	52. A
3. C	13. C	23. A	33. B	43. C	53. D
4. A	14. A	24. A	34. C	44. C	54. D
5. B	15. A	25. A	35. D	45. D	55. A
6. A	16. B	26. B	36. D	46. A	56. B
7. D	17. D	27. A	37. C	47. B	57. C
8. C	18. A	28. C	38. A	48. A	58. B
9. D	19. A	29. C	39. A	49. C	59. C
10. C	20. C	30. A	40. A	50. C	60. A

TEST 3

DIRECTIONS: The following test contains 60 questions to be completed in 11 minutes. The two lists below—the correct list on the left and the list to be checked on the right—are to be compared quickly and accurately in that time. Mark your answer A, B, C or D based on the following information:
Mark "A" if the two items are exactly the same (no errors)
Mark "B" if there is an error in the address only
Mark "C" if there is an error in the ZIP code only
Mark "D" if there are errors in both the address and ZIP code
PRINT THE LETTER OF THE CORRECT ANSWER IN THE SPACE AT THE RIGHT.

	CORRECT LIST		LIST TO BE CHECKED		
1.	405 Winter Rd. NW Albany, GA	31706	405 Winter Rd. NW Albany, NY	37106	1._____
2.	607 S. Calaveras Rd. Starkville, MS	39759	607 S. Calaveras Rd. Starkville, MS	39759	2._____
3.	8406 La Casa St. Martin, KY	41649	8406 La Casa St. Martin, KY	41649	3._____
4.	121 N. Rippon St. Haiku, HI	96708	121 N. Rippen St. Haiku, HI	96708	4._____
5.	226 Stoerner Ave. Wideman, AR	72585	226 Stoerner Ave. Wideman, AK	72535	5._____
6.	3790 Serge St. Sodus, NY	14551	3790 Serge St. Sodus, NY	14551	6._____
7.	3429 Hermosa Dr. Huntingdon, PA	16652	3429 Hermosa Dr. Huntingdon, PA	15662	7._____
8.	3628 S. Zeeland St. Baltimore, MD	21205	3628 S. Zeeland St. Baltimore, MD	21025	8._____
9.	1330 Cheverly Ave. Belmar, NJ	07715	1330 Cheverley Ave. Belmar, NJ	07715	9._____
10.	1689 N. Derwood Dr. Arco, ID	83213	1689 N. Derwood Rd. Arco, ID	83213	10._____
11.	388 Sunrise Ct. Lawrence, KS	66049	388 Sunrise Ct. Lawrence, KS	66049	11._____
12.	635 Lehigh La. Orlando, FL	32862	653 Lehigh La. Orlando, FL	32362	12._____
13.	2560 Lansford Pl. Albion, PA	16401	2560 Landsford Pl. Albion, PA	16411	13._____

49

14. 4631 Central Ave. Havre de Grace, MD	21078	4361 Central Ave. Havre de Grace, MD	21078	14._____
15. 24 Holiday Dr. Mason City, IA	50401	24 Holiday Dr. Mason City, IA	50701	15._____
16. 758 Los Arboles Ave. Bluffton, MN	56518	758 Los Arboles Ave. Bluffton, MN	56518	16._____
17. 3282 E. Downington St. Lynbrook, NY	11563	3282 E. Downington St. Lynbrook, NY	11563	17._____
18. 7117 Burlingham Ave. Tombstone, AZ	85638	7117 Burlingham Ave. Tombstone, AZ	85368	18._____
19. 32 Oaklawn Blvd. Syracuse, NY	13210	32 Oaklawn Blvd. Syracuse, NY	13210	19._____
20. 1274 Manzana Rd. Mesa, AZ	85207	1274 Manzona Rd. Mesa, AZ	80257	20._____
21. 4598 E. Kenilworth Dr. Logan, UT	84341	4598 E. Kenilworth Dr. Logan, UT	84341	21._____
22. 616 Berger Pl. Dayton, OK	73449	616 Berger Pl. Dayton, OK	73499	22._____
23. 1172 W. 83rd Ave. Louisville, KY	40298	1172 W. 83rd Ave. Louisville, KY	40298	23._____
24. 6434 E. Pulaski St. Atlantic City, NJ	08405	6434 E. Pulaski St. Atlantic City, NJ	08405	24._____
25. 2764 Rutherford Pl. Duluth, MN	55810	2674 Rutherford Pl. Duluth, MN	55810	25._____
26. 565 Greenville Blvd. Albany, NY	12222	565 Greenville Blvd. Albany, NY	12222	26._____
27. 319 Euclid Ave. Washington, DC	20013	391 Euclid Ave. Washington, DC	21003	27._____
28. 3824 Massasoit St. Honolulu, HI	96847	3824 Massasoit St. Honolulu, HI	96877	28._____
29. 22 Sagnaw Pkwy. Towson, MD	21286	22 Saginaw Pkwy. Towson, MD	21826	29._____
30. 2411 Chiofo Dr. Byram, CT	10573	2411 Chiofo Dr. Byram, CT	10753	30._____

31. 1928 S. Fairfield Ave. Ogden, AR	71853	1928 S. Farfield Ave. Ogden, AR	71853	31._____
32. 36218 Overhills Dr. Pensacola, FL	32597	36218 Overhills Dr. Pensacola, FL	32597	32._____
33. 5386 Fifth Ave. New York, NY	10025	5386 Fifth Ave. New York, NY	10025	33._____
34. 7526 Naraganset Pl. Paxico, KS	66526	7526 Naraganset Pl. Paxico, KS	65626	34._____
35. 52626 W. Oglesby Dr. Brooklyn, NY	11225	56226 W. Oglesby Dr. Brooklyn, NY	11235	35._____
36. 1003 Winchester Rd. Hershey, PA	17033	1003 Windchester Rd. Hershey, PA	17033	36._____
37. 347 Cavanaugh Ct. Covington, KY	41011	347 Cavanaugh Ct. Covington, KY	41011	37._____
38. 225 Robbins La. Kendall, CA	90551	225 Robbins La. Kendall, CA	90551	38._____
39. 225 El Camino Blvd. Sacramento, CA	95814	225 El Camino Blvd. Sacromento, CA	95844	39._____
40. 7310 Suncrest Dr. Wildwood, NJ	08260	7310 Suncrest Dr. Wildwood, NJ	08260	40._____
41. 1987 Wellington Ave. Roanoke, VA	24038	1897 Wellington Ave. Roanoke, VA	24088	41._____
42. 3124 S. 71st St. Altoona, PA	16601	3124 S. 71st St. Altoona, PA	16601	42._____
43. 729 Lincolnwood Blvd. Bloomington, IN	47401	729 Lincolnwood Blvd. Bloomington, IN	47401	43._____
44. 1166 N. Beaumont Dr. New Haven, CT	06533	1166 N. Beaumont Dr. New Maven, CT	06533	44._____
45. 3224 Winecona Pl. Norwalk, CT	06857	3224 Winecona Pl. Norwalk, CT	06357	45._____
46. 608 La Calle Bienvenida Madison, WI	53786	608 La Calle Bienvenida Madison, WI	53786	46._____
47. 808 Kinsella St. La Molte, IA	52045	808 Kinsella St. Le Molte, IA	52005	47._____

48.	8625 Armitage Ave. NW Buffalo, NY	14203	8625 Arnitage Ave. NW Buffalo, NY	12403	48._____
49.	2343 Broadview Ave. Syosset, NY	11791	2343 Broadview Ave. Syosset, NY	17191	49._____
50.	4279 Grand Ave. Wakefield, RI	02880	4279 Grand Ave. Weakfield, RI	02880	50._____
51.	165 32nd Ave. Iowa City, IA	52246	165 32nd Ave. Iowa City, IA	52246	51._____
52.	12742 N. Deerborn St. Milwaukee, WI	53217	12742 N. Deerborn St. Milwaukee, WI	53217	52._____
53.	114 Estancia Ave. Daytona Beach, FL	32198	114 Estancia Ave. Daytona Beach, FL	32198	53._____
54.	351 S. Berwyn Rd. Riverhead, NY	11901	351 S. Berywn Rd. Riverhead, NY	11191	54._____
55.	7732 Hollywood Ave. Miami, FL	33126	7732 Hollywood Blvd. Miami, FL	33126	55._____
56.	6337 C St. SW Savannah, GA	31406	6637 C St. SW Savannah, GA	31406	56._____
57.	57895 E. Drexyl Ave. Akron, OH	44301	57895 E. Drexyl Ave. Akron, OH	44301	57._____
58.	19891 Overberry La. Altro, TX	75923	19891 Overberry La. Altro, TX	75523	58._____
59.	3465 S. Nashville St. Evansville, IN	47732	3465 S. Nashville St. Evansville, ID	43772	59._____
60.	1226 Odell Blvd. Bethlehem, PA	18015	1226 Odell Blvd. Bethleham, PA	18105	60._____

KEY (CORRECT ANSWERS)

1. D	11. A	21. A	31. B	41. D	51. A
2. A	12. D	22. C	32. A	42. A	52. A
3. A	13. D	23. A	33. A	43. A	53. A
4. B	14. B	24. A	34. C	44. B	54. D
5. D	15. C	25. B	35. D	45. C	55. B
6. A	16. A	26. A	36. B	46. A	56. B
7. C	17. A	27. D	37. A	47. D	57. A
8. C	18. C	28. C	38. A	48. D	58. C
9. B	19. A	29. D	39. D	49. C	59. D
10. B	20. D	30. C	40. A	50. B	60. D

TEST 4

DIRECTIONS: The following test contains 60 questions to be completed in 11 minutes. The two lists below—the correct list on the left and the list to be checked on the right—are to be compared quickly and accurately in that time. Mark your answer A, B, C or D based on the following information:

Mark "A" if the two items are exactly the same (no errors)
Mark "B" if there is an error in the address only
Mark "C" if there is an error in the ZIP code only
Mark "D" if there are errors in both the address and ZIP code
PRINT THE LETTER OF THE CORRECT ANSWER IN THE SPACE AT THE RIGHT.

CORRECT LIST		LIST TO BE CHECKED		
1. 94002 Chappel Ct. Stamford, CT	06926	94002 Chappel Ct. Stamford, CT	06926	1._____
2. 512 La Vega Dr. Myrtle Beach, SC	29575	512 La Vega Dr. Myrtle Beach, SC	29575	2._____
3. 8774 W. Winona Pl. Columbia, SC	29201	8774 W. Winona Pl. Columbia, SC	29021	3._____
4. 6431 Ingleside St. Virginia Beach, VA	23450	6431 Ingleside St. Virginia Beach, VA	24350	4._____
5. 227 N. Leanington St. Providence, RI	02909	227 N. Leenington St. Providence, RI	02909	5._____
6. 2355 Estrada Blvd. New York, NY	11225	2335 Estrada Blvd. New York, NY	12225	6._____
7. 3987 E. Westwood Ave. Green Bay, WI	54304	3987 W. Eastwood Ave. Green Bay, WI	54034	7._____
8. 117 Appleseed Ct. Skamokawa, WA	98647	117 Appleseed Ct. Skamokawa, WA	99647	8._____
9. 2674 E. Champlain Cir. Quogue, NY	11959	2674 E. Champlain Cir. Quogue, NY	11959	9._____
10. 8751 Elmhurst Blvd. Ames, IA	50014	8751 Elmhurst Blvd. Amos, IA	50014	10._____
11. 664 Solano Dr. Erie, PA	16541	664 Solaro Dr. Erie, PA	16541	11._____
12. 4423 S. Escenaba St. Woonsocket, RI	02895	4423 S. Escanaba St. Woonsocket, RI	02895	12._____
13. 1198 N St. NW Canton, OH	44798	1198 N St. NW Canton, OH	44798	13._____

14. 4004 Kolb Ct. Sparta, GA	31087	4004 Kolb Ct. Sparta, GA	31087	14._____
15. 96753 Wrightwood Ave. Pawleys Island, SC	29585	96753 Wrightwood Ave. Pauleys Island, SC	25985	15._____
16. 2445 Sangamow Ave. North Valley Stream, NY	11580	2445 Sangamow Ave. North Valley Stream, NY	11580	16._____
17. 5117 E. 67th Pl. Seattle, WA	98198	5117 E. 67th St. Seattle, WA	99198	17._____
18. 847 Mesa Grande Pl. Ocala, FL	34477	847 Mesa Grande Pl. Ocala, FL	37744	18._____
19. 1100 Cermaken St. Waterford, CT	06385	1100 Cermaken St. Waterfort, CT	06685	19._____
20. 321 Tijeras Ave. NW Atlanta, GA	30301	321 Tijeras Ave. NW Atlanta, GA	30301	20._____
21. 3405 Prospect St. Olympia, WA	98501	3045 Prospect St. Olympia, WA	89501	21._____
22. 6643 Burlington Pl. Adams, TN	37010	6643 Burlington Pl. Adams, TN	37010	22._____
23. 851 Esperanza Blvd. Tully, NY	13159	851 Esparanza Blvd. Tully, NY	13199	23._____
24. 212 Marshall St. Jenkinjones, WV	24848	212 Marshall St. Jenkinjones, WV	24848	24._____
25. 1008 Pennsylvania Ave. Washington, DC	20002	1008 Pennsylvania Ave. Washington, DC	20008	25._____
26. 2924 26th St. N Great Falls, MT	59401	2924 26th St. N Great Falls, MT	59041	26._____
27. 7115 Highland Dr. Chattanooga, TN	37404	7115 Highland Dr. Chatanooga, TN	37404	27._____
28. 379 Francis Pkwy. Chaptico, MD	20621	379 Francis Pkwy. Chaptico, MA	20621	28._____
29. 3508 Camron Mills Rd. Gibson, PA	18820	3508 Camron Mills Rd. Gibson, PA	18820	29._____
30. 67158 Capston Dr. Morgantown, WV	26505	67158 Capston Dr. Morgantown, WV	26055	30._____

31. 3613 S. Taylor Ave. Acton, MT	59002	3613 S. Taylor Ave. Action, MT	58002	31._____
32. 2421 Menokin Dr. Coyote, NM	87012	2421 Menokin Dr. Coyote, NM	87012	32._____
33. 3226 M St. NW Durham, NC	27717	3226 N St. NW Durham, NC	27717	33._____
34. 1201 Court House Rd. Santa Fe, NM	87500	1201 Court House Rd. Santa Fe, NM	87500	34._____
35. 75 Caswell Pl. Findlay, OH	45840	75 Caswell Pl. Findley, OH	45340	35._____
36. 17 Bennett St. Media, PA	19091	17 Bennet St. Media, PA	19901	36._____
37. 7 Vine Bowl Dr. Adams, NE	68301	7 Wine Bowl Dr. Adams, NE	68801	37._____
38. 126 McKinley Ave. Raleigh, NC	27603	126 McKinley Ave. Raleigh, NC	27608	38._____
39. 384 Nepperhan Rd. Rochester, NY	14622	384 Nepperhan Rd. Rochester, NY	14622	39._____
40. 1077 Contreras Ave. Chicago, IL	60615	1077 Contreras Ave. Chicago, IL	60615	40._____
41. 111 Caroline Pl. Jackson, TN	38301	111 Caroline Pl. Jackson, TN	38001	41._____
42. 21 Greenleaf Blvd. Rye, NY	10580	21 Greenleaf Blvd. Rye, NJ	10580	42._____
43. 245 Rumsey Rd. Yonkers, NY	10705	245 Ramsey Rd. Yonkers, NY	10705	43._____
44. 927 South St. Peekskill, NY	10566	927 South St. Peekskill, NY	10656	44._____
45. 44 Monroe Ave. Larchmont, NY	10538	44 Monroe Ave. Larchmont, NY	10538	45._____
46. 39 Andrea La. Scarsdale, NY	10583	39 Andrea La. Scarsdale, NY	10588	46._____
47. 1006 Baumgartner Rd. Ruland, WY	62143	1006 Baumgardner Rd. Ruland, WY	62443	47._____

48. 51 Cypress Rd. New Hope, PA	18938	51 Cypress Rd. New Hape, PA	19938	48._____
49. 213 Shore Lane Rd. Elkton, MD	21922	213 Shore Lane Rd. Elkton, MD	21192	49._____
50. 189 Columbus Ave. Silver Spring, MD	20916	189 Columbus Ave. Silver Spring, MD	20916	50._____
51. 124 W. Stationery Rd. Beckley, WV	25801	124 W. Stationery Rd. Beckley, WV	25801	51._____
52. 650 Pinecrest Ct. Purdy, VT	03124	650 Pinecrest Ct. Purdy, VT	03124	52._____
53. 129 Tewksbury Rd. Mackinaw, IL	61755	129 Tewksbury Rd. Mackinaw, IN	61175	53._____
54. 100 Gallow Hill Rd. SW San Antonio, TX	78298	100 Gallow Hill Rd. SE San Antonio, TX	78288	54._____
55. 234 Myrtle Ave. Greensboro, NC	27499	234 Myrtle Ave. Greenboro, NC	27499	55._____
56. 35 Chase Pl. NE Cook, NE	68329	35 Chase Pl. NE Cooke, NC	68239	56._____
57. 14 Terrace Ave. Tyler, TX	75798	14 Terrace Ave. Tyler, TX	75798	57._____
58. 35 Collins Point Rd. Zephyr, TX	76890	35 Collins Point Rd. Zephyr, TX	76890	58._____
59. 164 Sagmor Ct. Omaha, NE	68197	164 Sagmor St. Omaha, NE	68797	59._____
60. 117 Warburton Dr. Oak Park, IL	60301	117 Warbarton Dr. Oak Park, IL	60801	60._____

KEY (CORRECT ANSWERS)

1. A	11. B	21. D	31. D	41. C	51. A
2. A	12. B	22. A	32. A	42. B	52. A
3. C	13. A	23. D	33. B	43. B	53. D
4. C	14. A	24. A	34. A	44. C	54. D
5. B	15. D	25. C	35. D	45. A	55. B
6. D	16. A	26. C	36. D	46. C	56. D
7. D	17. D	27. B	37. D	47. D	57. A
8. C	18. C	28. B	38. C	48. D	58. A
9. A	19. D	29. A	39. A	49. C	59. D
10. B	20. A	30. C	40. A	50. A	60. D

NAME AND NUMBER CHECKING

EXAMINATION SECTION
TEST 1

DIRECTIONS: Questions 1 through 17 consist of sets of names and addresses. In each question, the name and address in Column II should be an exact copy of the name and address in Column I.

If there is:
a mistake only in the name, mark your answer A;
a mistake only in the address, mark your answer B;
a mistake in both name and address, mark your answer C;
NO mistake in either name or address, mark your answer D.

SAMPLE QUESTION

Column I

Christina Magnusson
288 Greene Street
New York, N.Y. 10003

Column II

Christina Magnusson
288 Greene Street
New York, N.Y. 10013

Since there is a mistake only in the address (the zip code should be 10003 instead of 10013), the answer to the sample question is B.

COLUMN I	COLUMN II	
1. Ms. Joan Kelly 313 Franklin Ave. Brooklyn, N.Y. 11202	Ms. Joan Kielly 318 Franklin Ave. Brooklyn, N.Y. 11202	1.____
2. Mrs. Eileen Engel 47-24 86 Road Queens, N.Y. 11122	Mrs. Ellen Engel 47-24 86 Road Queens, N.Y. 11122	2.____
3. Marcia Michaels 213 E. 81 St. New York, N.Y. 10012	Marcia Michaels 213 E. 81 St. New York, N.Y. 10012	3.____
4. Rev. Edward J. Smyth 1401 Brandeis Street San Francisco, Calif. 96201	Rev. Edward J. Smyth 1401 Brandies Street San Francisco, Calif. 96201	4.____
5. Alicia Rodriguez 24-68 81 St. Elmhurst, N.Y. 11122	Alicia Rodriguez 2468 81 St. Elmhurst, N.Y. 11122	5.____
6. Ernest Eisemann 21 Columbia St. New York, N.Y. 10007	Ernest Eisermann 21 Columbia St. New York, N.Y. 10007	6.____

Column I	COLUMN II	
7. Mr. & Mrs. George Petersson 87-11 91st Avenue Woodhaven, N.Y. 11421	Mr. & Mrs. George Peterson 87-11 91st Avenue Woodhaven, N.Y. 11421	7.____
8. Mr. Ivan Klebnikov 1848 Newkirk Avenue Brooklyn, N.Y. 11226	Mr. Ivan Klebikov 1848 Newkirk Avenue Brooklyn, N.Y. 11622	8.____
9. Samuel Rothfleisch 71 Pine Street New York, N.Y. 10005	Samuel Rothfleisch 71 Pine Street New York, N.Y. 10005	9.____
10. Mrs. Isabel Tonnessen 198 East 185th Street Bronx, N.Y. 10458	Mrs. Isabel Tonnessen 189 East 185th Street Bronx, N.Y. 10458	10.____
11. Esteban Perez 173 Eighth Street Staten Island, N.Y. 10306	Estaban Perez 173 Eighth Street Staten Island, N.Y. 10306	11.____
12. Esta Wong 141 West 68 St. New York, N.Y. 10023	Esta Wang 141 West 68 St. New York, N.Y. 10023	12.____
13. Dr. Alberto Grosso 3475 12th Avenue Brooklyn, N.Y. 11218	Dr. Alberto Grosso 3475 12th Avenue Brooklyn, N.Y. 11218	13.____
14. Mrs. Ruth Bortlas 482 Theresa Ct. Far Rockaway, N.Y. 11691	Ms. Ruth Bortlas 482 Theresa Ct. Far Rockaway, N.Y. 11169	14.____
15. Mr. & Mrs. Howard Fox 2301 Sedgwick Ave. Bronx, N.Y. 10468	Mr. & Mrs. Howard Fox 231 Sedgwick Ave. Bronx, N.Y. 10468	15.____
16. Miss Marjorie Black 223 East 23 Street New York, N.Y. 10010	Miss Margorie Black 223 East 23 Street New York, N.Y. 10010	16.____
17. Michelle Herman 806 Valley Rd. Old Tappan, N.J. 07675	Michelle Hermann 806 Valley Dr. Old Tappan, N.J. 07675	17.____

KEY (CORRECT ANSWERS)

1.	C		6.	A
2.	A		7.	A
3.	D		8.	C
4.	B		9.	D
5.	B		10.	B

11.	A
12.	A
13.	D
14.	C
15.	B
16.	A
17.	C

TEST 2

DIRECTIONS: Questions 1 through 15 are to be answered SOLELY on the instructions given below. *PRINT THE LETTER OF THE CORRECT ANSWER IN THE SPACE AT THE RIGHT.*

INSTRUCTIONS:

In each of the following questions, the 3-line name and address in Column I is the master-list entry, and the 3-line entry in Column 2 is the information to be checked against the master list. If there is one line that does not match, mark your answer A; if there are two lines that do not match, mark your answer B; if all three lines do not match, mark your answer C; if the lines all match exactly, mark your answer D.

SAMPLE QUESTION

Column I
Mark L. Field
11-09 Prince Park Blvd.
Bronx, N.Y. 11402

Column II
Mark L. Field
11-99 Prince Park Way
Bronx, N.Y. 11401

The first lines in each column match exactly. The second lines do not match since 11-09 does not match 11-99; and Blvd. does not match Way. The third lines do not match either since 11402 does not match 11401. Therefore, there are two lines that do not match, and the CORRECT answer is B.

COLUMN I	COLUMN II	
1. Jerome A. Jackson 1243 14th Avenue New York, N.Y. 10023	Jerome A. Johnson 1234 14th Avenue New York, N.Y. 10023	1.___
2. Sophie Strachtheim 33-28 Connecticut Ave. Far Rockaway, N.Y. 11697	Sophie Strachtheim 33-28 Connecticut Ave. Far Rockaway, N.Y. 11697	2.___
3. Elisabeth N.T. Gorrell 256 Exchange St. New York, N.Y. 10013	Elizabeth N.T. Gorrell 256 Exchange St. New York, N.Y. 10013	3.___
4. Maria J. Gonzalez 7516 E. Sheepshead Rd. Brooklyn, N.Y. 11240	Maria J. Gonzalez 7516 N. Shepshead Rd. Brooklyn, N.Y. 11240	4.___
5. Leslie B. Brautenweiler 21 57A Seiler Terr. Flushing, N.Y. 11367	Leslie B. Brautenwieler 21-75A Seiler Terr. Flushing, N.J. 11367	5.___
6. Rigoberto J. Peredes 157 Twin Towers, #18F Tottenville, S.I., N.Y.	Rigoberto J. Peredes 157 Twin Towers, #18F Tottenville, S.I., N.Y.	6.___

COLUMN I	COLUMN II	
7. Pietro F. Albino P.O. Box 7548 Floral Park, N.Y. 11005	Pietro F. Albina P.O. Box 7458 Floral Park, N.Y. 11005	7._____
8. Joanne Zimmermann Bldg. SW, Room 314 532-4601	Joanne Zimmermann Bldg. SW, Room 314 532-4601	8._____
9. Carlyle Whetstone Payroll Div.-A, Room 212A 262-5000, ext. 471	Caryle Whetstone Payroll Div.-A, Room 212A 262-5000, ext. 417	9._____
10. Kenneth Chiang Legal Council, Room 9745 (201) 416-9100, ext. 17	Kenneth Chiang Legal Counsel, Room 9745 (201) 416-9100, ext. 17	10._____
11. Ethel Koenig Personnel Services Division, Room 433; 635-7572	Ethel Hoenig Personal Services Division, Room 433; 635-7527	11._____
12. Joyce Ehrhardt Office of the Administrator, Room W56; 387-8706	Joyce Ehrhart Office of the Administrator, Room W56; 387-7806	12._____
13. Ruth Lang EAM Bldg., Room C101 625-2000, ext. 765	Ruth Lang EAM Bldg., Room C110 625-2000, ext. 765	13._____
14. Anne Marie Ionozzi Investigations, Room 827 576-4000, ext. 832	Anna Marie Ionozzi Investigation, Room 827 566-4000, ext. 832	14._____
15. Willard Jameson Fm C Bldg., Room 687 454-3010	Willard Jamieson Fm C Bldg., Room 687 454-3010	15._____

———

KEY (CORRECT ANSWERS)

1.	B	6.	D
2.	D	7.	B
3.	A	8.	D
4.	A	9.	B
5.	C	10.	A

11.	C
12.	B
13.	A
14.	C
15.	A

———

TEST 3

DIRECTIONS: Questions 1 through 10 are to be answered on the basis of the following instructions. *PRINT THE LETTER OF THE CORRECT ANSWER IN THE SPACE AT THE RIGHT.*

INSTRUCTIONS:

For each such set of names, addresses, and numbers listed in Columns I and II, select your answer from the following options:

- A. The names in Columns I and II are different.
- B. The addresses in Columns I and II are different.
- C. The numbers in Columns I and II are different.
- D. The names, addresses, and numbers in Columns I and II are identical.

COLUMN I	COLUMN II	
1. Francis Jones 62 Stately Avenue 96-12446	Francis Jones 62 Stately Avenue 96-21446	1.____
2. Julio Montez 19 Ponderosa Road 56-73161	Julio Montez 19 Ponderosa Road 56-71361	2.____
3. Mary Mitchell 2314 Melbourne Drive 68-92172	Mary Mitchell 2314 Melbourne Drive 68-92172	3.____
4. Harry Patterson 25 Dunne Street 14-33430	Harry Patterson 25 Dunne Street 14-34330	4.____
5. Patrick Murphy 171 West Hosmer Street 93-81214	Patrick Murphy 171 West Hosmer Street 93-18214	5.____
6. August Schultz 816 St. Clair Avenue 53-40149	August Schultz 816 St. Claire Avenue 53-40149	6.____
7. George Taft 72 Runnymede Street 47-04033	George Taft 72 Runnymede Street 47-04023	7.____
8. Angus Henderson 1418 Madison Street 81-76375	Angus Henderson 1418 Madison Street 81-76375	8.____
9. Carolyn Mazur 12 Riverview Road 38-99615	Carolyn Mazur 12 Rivervane ftoad 38-99615	9.____

<u>COLUMN I</u>   <u>COLUMN II</u>

10. Adele Russell   Adela Russell   10.____
     1725 Lansing Lane   1725 Lansing Lane
     72-91962   72-91962

———

KEY (CORRECT ANSWERS)

1.	C	6.	B
2.	C	7.	C
3.	D	8.	D
4.	C	9.	B
5.	C	10.	A

———

TEST 4

DIRECTIONS: Questions 1 through 20 test how good you are at catching mistakes in typing or printing. In each question, the name and address in Column II should be an exact copy of the name and address in Column I. Mark your answer

- A. if there is no mistake in either name or address;
- B. if there is a mistake in both name and address;
- C. if there is a mistake only in the name;
- D. if there is a mistake only in the address.

PRINT THE LETTER OF THE CORRECT ANSWER IN THE SPACE AT THE RIGHT.

COLUMN I	COLUMN II	
1. Milos Yanocek 33-60 14 Street Long Island City, N.Y. 11011	Milos Yanocek 33-60 14 Street Long Island City, N.Y. 11001	1._____
2. Alphonse Sabattelo 24 Minnetta Lane New York, N.Y. 10006	Alphonse Sabbattelo 24 Minetta Lane New York, N.Y. 10006	2._____
3. Helen Steam 5 Metropolitan Oval Bronx, N.Y. 10462	Helene Stearn 5 Metropolitan Oval Bronx, N.Y. 10462	3._____
4. Jacob Weisman 231 Francis Lewis Boulevard Forest Hills, N.Y. 11325	Jacob Weisman 231 Francis Lewis Boulevard Forest Hills, N.Y. 11325	4._____
5. Riccardo Fuente 134 West 83 Street New York, N.Y. 10024	Riccardo Fuentes 134 West 88 Street New York, N.Y. 10024	5._____
6. Dennis Lauber 52 Avenue D Brooklyn, N.Y. 11216	Dennis Lauder 52 Avenue D Brooklyn, N.Y. 11216	6._____
7. Paul Cutter 195 Galloway Avenue Staten Island, N.Y. 10356	Paul Cutter 175 Galloway Avenue Staten Island, N.Y. 10365	7._____
8. Sean Donnelly 45-58 41 Avenue Woodside, N.Y. 11168	Sean Donnelly 45-58 41 Avenue Woodside, N.Y. 11168	8._____
9. Clyde Willot 1483 Rockaway Avenue Brooklyn, N.Y. 11238	Clyde Willat 1483 Rockway Avenue Brooklyn, N.Y. 11238	9._____

COLUMN I	COLUMN II	
10. Michael Stanakis 419 Sheriden Avenue Staten Island, N.Y. 10363	Michael Stanakis 419 Sheraden Avenue Staten Island, N.Y. 10363	10.____
11. Joseph DiSilva 63-84 Saunders Road Rego Park, N.Y. 11431	Joseph Disilva 64-83 Saunders Road Rego Park, N.Y. 11431	11.____
12. Linda Polansky 2225 Fenton Avenue Bronx, N.Y. 10464	Linda Polansky 2255 Fenton Avenue Bronx, N.Y. 10464	12.____
13. Alfred Klein 260 Hillside Terrace Staten Island, N.Y. 15545	Alfred Klein 260 Hillside Terrace Staten Island, N.Y. 15545	13.____
14. William McDonnell 504 E. 55 Street New York, N.Y. 10103	William McConnell 504 E. 55 Street New York, N.Y. 10108	14.____
15. Angela Cipolla 41-11 Parson Avenue Flushing, N.Y. 11446	Angela Cipola 41-11 Parsons Avenue Flushing, N.Y. 11446	15.____
16. Julie Sheridan 1212 Ocean Avenue Brooklyn, N.Y. 11237	Julia Sheridan 1212 Ocean Avenue Brooklyn, N.Y. 11237	16.____
17. Arturo Rodriguez 2156 Cruger Avenue Bronx, N.Y. 10446	Arturo Rodrigues 2156 Cruger Avenue Bronx, N.Y. 10446	17.____
18. Helen McCabe 2044 East 19 Street Brooklyn, N.Y. 11204	Helen McCabe 2040 East 19 Street Brooklyn,. N.Y. 11204	18.____
19. Charles Martin 526 West 160 Street New York, N.Y. 10022	Charles Martin 526 West 160 Street New York, N.Y. 10022	19.____
20. Morris Rabinowitz 31 Avenue M Brooklyn, N.Y. 11216	Morris Rabinowitz 31 Avenue N Brooklyn, N.Y. 11216	20.____

KEY (CORRECT ANSWERS)

1.	D		11.	B
2.	B		12.	D
3.	C		13.	A
4.	A		14.	B
5.	B		15.	B
6.	C		16.	C
7.	D		17.	C
8.	A		18.	D
9.	B		19.	A
10.	D		20.	D

TEST 5

DIRECTIONS: In copying the addresses below from Column A to the same line in Column B, an Agent-in-Training made some errors. For Questions 1 through 5, if you find that the Agent made an error in

only one line, mark your answer A;
only two lines, mark your answer B;
only three lines, mark your answer C;
all four lines, mark your answer D.

EXAMPLE

Column A	Column B
24 Third Avenue	24 Third Avenue
5 Lincoln Road	5 Lincoln Street
50 Central Park West	6 Central Park West
37-21 Queens Boulevard	21-37 Queens Boulevard

Since errors were made on only three lines, namely the second, third, and fourth, the CORRECT answer is C.
PRINT THE LETTER OF THE CORRECT ANSWER IN THE SPACE AT THE RIGHT.

	Column A	Column B	
1.	57-22 Springfield Boulevard	75-22 Springfield Boulevard	1.____
	94 Gun Hill Road	94 Gun Hill Avenue	
	8 New Dorp Lane	8 New Drop Lane	
	36 Bedford Avenue	36 Bedford Avenue	
2.	538 Castle Hill Avenue	538 Castle Hill Avenue	2.____
	54-15 Beach Channel Drive	54-15 Beach Channel Drive	
	21 Ralph Avenue	21 Ralph Avenue	
	162 Madison Avenue	162 Morrison Avenue	
3.	49 Thomas Street	49 Thomas Street	3.____
	27-21 Northern Blvd.	21-27 Northern Blvd.	
	86 125th Street	86 125th Street	
	872 Atlantic Ave.	872 Baltic Ave.	
4.	261-17 Horace Harding Expwy.	261-17 Horace Harding Pkwy.	4.____
	191 Fordham Road	191 Fordham Road	
	6 Victory Blvd.	6 Victoria Blvd.	
	552 Oceanic Ave.	552 Ocean Ave.	
5.	90-05 38th Avenue	90-05 36th Avenue	5.____
	19 Central Park West	19 Central Park East	
	9281 Avenue X	9281 Avenue X	
	22 West Farms Square	22 West Farms Square	

KEY (CORRECT ANSWERS)

1. C
2. A
3. B
4. C
5. B

———

TEST 6

Questions 1-10.

DIRECTIONS: For Questions 1 through 10, choose the letter in Column II next to the number which EXACTLY matches the number in Column I. *PRINT THE LETTER OF THE CORRECT ANSWER IN THE SPACE AT THE RIGHT.*

<u>COLUMN I</u>   <u>COLUMN II</u>

1. 14235   A. 13254   1.____
                                     B. 12435
                                     C. 13245
                                     D. 14235

2. 70698   A. 90768   2.____
                                     B. 60978
                                     C. 70698
                                     D. 70968

3. 11698   A. 11689   3.____
                                     B. 11986
                                     C. 11968
                                     D. 11698

4. 50497   A. 50947   4.____
                                     B. 50497
                                     C. 50749
                                     D. 54097

5. 69635   A. 60653   5.____
                                     B. 69630
                                     C. 69365
                                     D. 69635

6. 1201022011   A. 1201022011   6.____
                                     B. 1201020211
                                     C. 1202012011
                                     D. 1021202011

7. 3893981389   A. 3893891389   7.____
                                     B. 3983981389
                                     C. 3983891389
                                     D. 3893981389

8. 4765476589   A. 4765476598   8.____
                                     B. 4765476588
                                     C. 4765476589
                                     D. 4765746589

COLUMN I   COLUMN II

9. 8679678938   A. 8679687938   9.____
                                      B. 8679678938
                                      C. 8697678938
                                      D. 8678678938

10. 6834836932   A. 6834386932   10.____
                                      B. 6834836923
                                      C. 6843836932
                                      D. 6834836932

Questions 11-15.

DIRECTIONS: For Questions 11 through 15, determine how many of the symbols in Column
             Z are exactly the same as the symbol in Column Y.
             If none is exactly the same, answer A;
             if only one symbol is exactly the same, answer B;
             if two symbols are exactly the same, answer C;
             if three symbols are exactly the same, answer D.

COLUMN Y   COLUMN Z

11. A123B1266   A123B1366   11.____
                                     A123B1266
                                     A133B1366
                                     A123B1266

12. CC28D3377   CD22D3377   12.____
                                     CC38D3377
                                     CC28C3377
                                     CC28D2277

13. M21AB201X   M12AB201X   13.____
                                     M21AB201X
                                     M21AB201Y
                                     M21BA201X

14. PA383Y744   AP383Y744   14.____
                                     PA338Y744
                                     PA388Y744
                                     PA383Y774

15. PB2Y8893   PB2Y8893   15.____
                                     PB2Y8893
                                     PB3Y8898
                                     PB2Y8893

_____

KEY (CORRECT ANSWERS)

1.	D	6.	A
2.	C	7.	D
3.	D	8.	C
4.	B	9.	B
5.	D	10.	D

11.	C
12.	A
13.	B
14.	A
15.	D

NAME AND NUMBER CHECKING
EXAMINATION SECTION
TEST 1

DIRECTIONS: Each question or incomplete statement is followed by several suggested answers or completions. Select the one that *BEST* answers the question or completes the statement. *PRINT THE LETTER OF THE CORRECT ANSWER IN THE SPACE AT THE RIGHT.*

Questions 1-10

DIRECTIONS: Questions 1 through 10 below present the identification numbers, initials, and last names of employees enrolled in a city retirement system. You are to choose the option (A, B, C, or D) that has the *identical* identification number, initials, and last name as those given in each question.

SAMPLE QUESTION
B145698 JL Jones
   A. B146798 JL Jones
   C. P145698 JL Jones

   B. B145698 JL Jonas
   D. B145698 JL Jones

The correct answer is D. Only option D shows the identification number, initials and last name exactly as they are in the sample question. Options A, B, and C have errors in the identification number or last name.

1. J297483 PL Robinson   1.____

   A. J294783 PL Robinson
   C. J297483 PI Robinson

   B. J297483 PL Robinson
   D. J297843 PL Robinson

2. S497662 JG Schwartz   2.____

   A. S497662 JG Schwarz
   C. S497662 JG Schwartz

   B. S497762 JG Schwartz
   D. S497663 JG Schwartz

3. G696436 LN Alberton   3.____

   A. G696436 LM Alberton
   C. G696346 LN Albertson

   B. G696436 LN Albertson
   D. G696436 LN Alberton

4. R774923 AD Aldrich   4.____

   A. R774923 AD Aldrich
   C. R774932 AP Aldrich

   B. R744923 AD Aldrich
   D. R774932 AD Allrich

5. N239638 RP Hrynyk   5.____

   A. N236938 PR Hrynyk
   C. N239638 PR Hrynyk

   B. N236938 RP Hrynyk
   D. N239638 RP Hrynyk

6. R156949 LT Carlson   6.____

   A. R156949 LT Carlton
   C. R159649 LT Carlton

   B. R156494 LT Carlson
   D. R156949 LT Carlson

7. T524697 MN Orenstein   7.____

    A.   T524697 MN Orenstein   B.   T524967 MN Orinstein
    C.   T524697 NM Ornstein   D.   T524967 NM Orenstein

8. L346239 JD Remsen   8.____

    A.   L346239 JD Remson   B.   L364239 JD Remsen
    C.   L346329 JD Remsen   D.   L346239 JD Remsen

9. P966438 SB Rieperson   9.____

    A.   P996438 SB Reiperson   B.   P966438 SB Reiperson
    C.   R996438 SB Rieperson   D.   P966438 SB Rieperson

10. D749382 CD Thompson   10.____

    A.   P749382 CD Thompson   B.   D749832 CD Thomsonn
    C.   D749382 CD Thompson   D.   D749823 CD Thomspon

Questions 11 - 20

DIRECTIONS: Each of Questions 11 through 20 gives the identification number and name of
a person who has received treatment at a certain hospital. You are to choose
the option (A, B, C, or D) which has *EXACTLY* the same identification number
and name as those given in the question.

SAMPLE QUESTION

123765 Frank Y. Jones   A.   123675 Frank Y. Jones
                                  B.   123765 Frank T. Jones
                                  C.   123765 Frank Y. Johns
                                  D.   123765 Frank Y. Jones

The correct answer is D. Only option D shows the identification number and name
exactly as they are in the sample question. Option A has a mistake in the identification number. Option B has a mistake in the middle initial of the name. Option C has a mistake in the
last name.

Now answer Questions 11 through 20 in the same manner.

11. 754898 Diane Malloy   A.   745898 Diane Malloy   11.____
                                    B.   754898 Dion Malloy
                                    C.   754898 Diane Malloy
                                    D.   754898 Diane Maloy

12. 661818 Ferdinand Figueroa   A.   661818 Ferdinand Figeuroa   12.____
                                    B.   661618 Ferdinand Figueroa
                                    C.   661818 Ferdnand Figueroa
                                    D.   661818 Ferdinand Figueroa

13. 100101 Norman D. Braustein   A.   100101 Norman D. Braustein   13.____
                                    B.   101001 Norman D. Braustein
                                    C.   100101 Norman P. Braustien
                                    D.   100101 Norman D. Bruastein

14. 838696 Robert Kittredge

   A. 838969 Robert Kittredge
   B. 838696 Robert Kittredge
   C. 388696 Robert Kittredge
   D. 838696 Robert Kittridge

14.____

15. 243716 Abraham Soletsky

   A. 243716 Abrahm Soletsky
   B. 243716 Abraham Solestky
   C. 243176 Abraham Soletsky
   D. 243716 Abraham Soletsky

15.____

16. 981121 Phillip M. Maas

   A. 981121 Phillip M. Mass
   B. 981211 Phillip M. Maas
   C. 981121 Phillip M. Maas
   D. 981121 Phillip N. Maas

16.____

17. 786556 George Macalusso

   A. 785656 George Macalusso
   B. 786556 George Macalusso
   C. 786556 George Maculasso
   D. 786556 George Macluasso

17.____

18. 639472 Eugene Weber

   A. 639472 Eugene Weber
   B. 639472 Eugene Webre
   C. 693472 Eugene Weber
   D. 639742 Eugene Weber

18.____

19. 724936 John J. Lomonaco

   A. 724936 John J. Lomanoco
   B. 724396 John J. Lomonaco
   C. 724936 John J. Lomonaco
   D. 724936 John J. Lamonaco

19.____

20. 899868 Michael Schnitzer

   A. 899868 Micheal Schnitzer
   B. 898968 Michael Schnizter
   C. 899688 Michael Schnitzer
   D. 899868 Michael Schnitzer

20.____

Questions: 21 - 28

DIRECTIONS: Questions 21 through 28 consist of lines of names, dates, and numbers which represent the names. membership dates, social security numbers, and members of the retirement system. For each question you are to choose the option (A, B, C, or D) in Column II which *EXACTLY* matches the information in Column I.

SAMPLE QUESTION

Column I

Crossen 12/23/56 173568929 253492

Column II

A. Crossen 2/23/56 173568929 253492
B. Crossen 12/23/56 173568729 253492
C. Crossen 12/23/56 173568929 253492
D. Crossan 12/23/56 173568929 258492

The correct answer is C. Only option C shows the name, date, and numbers exactly as they are in Column I. Option A has a mistake in the date. Option B has a mistake in the social security number. Option D has a mistake in the name and in the membership number.

21. Figueroa 1/15/64 119295386 147563   21.___

    A. Figueroa   1/5/64   119295386   147563
    B. Figueroa   1/15/64   119295386   147563
    C. Figueroa   1/15/64   119295836   147563
    D. Figueroa   1/15/64   119295886   147563

22. Goodridge 6/19/59 106237869 128352   22.___

    A. Goodridge   6/19/59   106287869   128332
    B. Goodrigde   6/19/59   106237869   128352
    C. Goodridge   6/9/59   106237869   128352
    D. Goodridge   6/19/59   106237869   128352

23. Balsam 9/13/57 109652382 116938   23.___

    A. Balsan   9/13/57   109652382   116938
    B. Balsam   9/13/57   109652382   116938
    C. Balsom   9/13/57   109652382   116938
    D. Balsalm   9/13/57   109652382   116938

24. Mackenzie 2/16/49 127362513 101917   24.___

    A. Makenzie   2/16/49   127362513   101917
    B. Mackenzie   2/16/49   127362513   101917
    C. Mackenzie   2/16/49   127362513   101977
    D. Mackenzie   2/16/49   127862513   101917

25. Halpern 12/2/73 115206359 286070   25.___

    A. Halpern   12/2/73   115206359   286070
    B. Halpern   12/2/73   113206359   286070
    C. Halpern   12/2/73   115206359   206870
    D. Halpern   12/2/73   115206359   286870

26. Phillips 4/8/66 137125516 192612   26.___

    A. Phillips   4/8/66   137125516   196212
    B. Philipps   4/8/66   137125516   192612
    C. Phillips   4/8/66   137125516   192612
    D. Phillips   4/8/66   137122516   192612

27. Francisce 11/9/63 123926037 152210   27.___

    A. Francisce   11/9/63   123826837   152210
    B. Francisce   11/9/63   123926037   152210
    C. Francisce   11/9/63   123936037   152210
    D. Franscice   11/9/63   123926037   152210

28. Silbert 7/28/54 118421999 178514   28.____

	Silbert	7/28/54	118421999	178544
A.	Silbert	7/28/54	118421999	178544
B.	Silbert	7/28/54	184421999	178514
C.	Silbert	7/28/54	118421999	178514
D.	Siblert	7/28/54	118421999	178514

KEY (CORRECT ANSWERS)

1.	B		16.	C
2.	C		17.	B
3.	D		18.	A
4.	A		19.	C
5.	D		20.	D
6.	D		21.	B
7.	A		22.	D
8.	D		23.	B
9.	D		24.	B
10.	C		25.	A
11.	C		26.	C
12.	D		27.	B
13.	A		28.	C
14.	B			
15.	D			

TEST 2

Questions 1-3

DIRECTIONS: Items 1 to 3 are a test of your proofreading ability. Each item consists of Copy I and Copy II. You are to assume that Copy I in each item is correct. Copy II, which is meant to be a duplicate of Copy I, may contain some typographical errors. In each item, compare Copy II with Copy I and determine the number of errors in Copy II. If there are:
no errors, mark your answer A;
1 or 2 errors, mark your answer B;
3 or 4 errors, mark your answer C;
5 or 6 errors, mark your answer D;
7 errors or more, mark your answer E.

1.   1.____

COPY I

The Commissioner, before issuing any such license, shall cause an investigation to be made of the premises named and described in such application, to determine whether all the provisions of the sanitary code, building code, state industrial code, state minimum wage law, local laws, regulations of municipal agencies, and other requirements of this article are fully observed. (Section B32-169.0 of Article 23.)

COPY II

The Commissioner, before issuing any such license shall cause an investigation to be made of the premises named and described in such applecation, to determine whether all the provisions of the sanitary code, bilding code, state industrial code, state minimum wage laws, local laws, regulations of municipal agencies, and other requirements of this article are fully observed. (Section E32-169.0 of Article 23.)

2.   2.____

COPY I

Among the persons who have been appointed to various agencies are John Queen, 9 West 55th Street, Brooklyn; Joseph Blount, 2497 Durward Road, Bronx: Lawrence K. Eberhardt, 3194 Bedford Street, Manhattan; Reginald L. Darcy, 1476 Allerton Drive, Bronx; and Benjamin Ledwith, 177 Greene Street, Manhattan.

COPY II

Among the persons who have been appointed to various agencies are John Queen, 9 West 56th Street, Brooklyn, Joseph Blount, 2497 Dureward Road, Bronx: Lawrence K. Eberhart , 3194 Belford Street, Manhattan; Reginald L. Barcey, 1476 Allerton drive, Bronx; and Benjamin Ledwith, 177 Green Street, Manhattan.

3.   3.____

COPY I

Except as hereinafter provided, it shall be unlawful to use, store or have on hand any inflammable motion picture film in quantities greater than one standard or two sub-standard reels, or aggregating more than two thousand feet in length, or more than ten pounds in weight without the permit required by this section.

COPY II

Except as herinafter provided, it shall be unlawfull to use, store or have on hand any inflamable motion picture film, in quantities greater than one standard or two substandard reels or aggregating more than two thousand feet in length, or more then ten pounds in weight without the permit required by this section.

Questions 4-6

Questions 4 to 6 are a test of your proofreading ability. Each question consists of Copy I and Copy II. You are to assume that Copy I in each question is correct. Copy II, which is meant to be a duplicate of Copy I, may contain some typographical errors. In each question, compare Copy II with Copy I and determine the number of errors in Copy II. If there are

no errors, mark your answer A;
1 or 2 errors, mark your answer B;
3 or 4 errors, mark your answer C;
5 errors or more, mark your answer D.

4.   4.____

COPY I

It shall be unlawful to install wires or appliances for electric light, heat or power, operating at a potential in excess of seven hundred fifty volts, in or on any part of a building, with the exception of a central station, sub-station, transformer, or switching vault, or motor room; provided, however, that the Commissioner may authorize the use of radio transmitting apparatus under special conditions.

COPY II

It shall be unlawful to install wires or appliances for electric light, heat or power, operating at a potential in excess of seven hundred fifty volts, in or on any part of a building, with the exception of a central station, sub-station, transformer, or switching vault, or motor room, provided, however, that the Commissioner may authorize the use of radio transmitting apperatus under special conditions.

5.   5.____

COPY I

The grand total debt service for the fiscal year 2006-07 amounts to $350,563,718.63, as compared with $309,561,347.27 for the current fiscal year, or an increase of $41,002,371.36. The amount payable from other sources in 2006-07 shows an increase of $13,264,165.47, resulting in an increase of $27,733,205.89 payable from tax levy funds.

COPY II

The grand total debt service for the fiscal year 2006-07 amounts to $350,568,718.63, as compared with $309,561,347.27 for the current fiscel year, or an increase of $41,002,371.36. The amount payable from other sources in 2006-07 show an increase of $13,264,165.47 resulting in an increase of $27,733,295.89 payable from tax levy funds.

6.

COPY I

The following site proposed for the new building is approximately rectangular in shape and comprises an entire block, having frontages of about 721 feet on 16th Road, 200 feet on 157th Street, 721 feet on 17th Avenue and 200 feet on 154th Street, with a gross area of about 144,350 square feet. The 2006-07 assessed valuation is $28,700,000 of which $6,000,000 is for improvements.

COPY II

The following site proposed for the new building is approximately rectangular in shape and comprises an entire block, having frontage of about 721 feet on 16th Road, 200 feet on 157th Street, 721 feet on 17th Avenue, and 200 feet on 134th Street, with a gross area of about 114,350 square feet. The 2006-07 assessed valuation is $28,700,000 of which $6,000,000 is for improvements.

———

KEY (CORRECT ANSWERS)

1. D
2. E
3. E
4. B
5. D
6. C

———

TEST 3

Questions 1-8

DIRECTIONS: Each of the Questions numbered 1 through 8 consists of three sets of names and name codes. In each question, the two names and name codes on the same line are supposed to be exactly the same.

Look carefully at each set of names and codes and mark your answer

- A. if there are mistakes in all three sets
- B. if there are mistakes in two of the sets
- C. if there is a mistake in only one set
- D. if there are no mistakes in any of the sets

SAMPLE QUESTION

The following sample question is given to help you understand the procedure

Macabe, John N. - V 53162	Macade, John N. - V 53162
Howard, Joan S. - J 24791	Howard, Joan S. - J 24791
Ware, Susan B. - A 45068	Ware, Susan B. - A 45968

In the above sample question, the names and name codes of the first set are not exactly the same because of the spelling of the last name (Macabe - Macade). The names and name codes of the second set are exactly the same. The names and name codes of the third set are not exactly the same because the two name codes are different (A 45068 - A 45968). Since there are mistakes in only 2 of the sets, the answer to the sample question is B.

1. Powell, Michael C. - 78537 F   Powell, Michael C. - 78537 F   1.____
    Martinez, Pablo J. - 24435 P   Martinez, Pablo J. - 24435 P
    MacBane, Eliot M. - 98674 E   MacBane, Eliot M. - 98674 E

2. Fitz-Kramer Machines Inc.   Fitz-Kramer Machines Inc.   2.____
        - 259090   - 259090
    Marvel Cleaning Service   Marvel Cleaning Service
        - 482657   - 482657
    Donato, Carl G. - 637418   Danato, Carl G. - 687418

3. Martin Davison Trading Corp.   Martin Davidson Trading Corp.   3.____
        - 43108 T   - 43108 T
    Cotwald Lighting Fixtures   Cotwald Lighting Fixtures
        - 76065 L   - 70056 L
    R. Crawford Plumbers   R. Crawford Plumbers
        - 23157 C   - 23157 G

4. Fraiman Engineering Corp.
   - M4773
   Neuman, Walter B. - N7745
   Pierce, Eric M. - W6304

Friaman Engineering Corp.
   - M4773
Neumen, Walter B. - N7745
Pierce, Eric M. - W6304

4.____

5. Constable, Eugene - B 64837
   Derrick, Paul - H 27119
   Heller, Karen - S 49606

Comstable, Eugene - B 64837
Derrik, Paul - H 27119
Heller, Karen - S 46906

5.____

6. Hernando Delivery Service Co.
   - D 7456
   Barettz Electrical Supplies
   - N 5392
   Tanner, Abraham - M 4798

Hernando Delivery Service Co.
   - D 7456
Barettz Electrical Supplies
   - N 5392
Tanner, Abraham - M 4798

6.____

7. Kalin Associates - R 38641
   Sealey, Robert E. - P 63533
   Seals! Office Furniture
   - R36742

Kaline Associates - R 38641
Sealey, Robert E. - P 63553
Seals! Office Furniture
   - R36742

7.____

8. Janowsky, Philip M.- 742213
   Hansen, Thomas H. - 934816
   L. Lester and Son Inc.
   - 294568

Janowsky, Philip M.- 742213
Hanson, Thomas H. - 934816
L. Lester and Son Inc.
   - 294568

8.____

Questions 9-13

DIRECTIONS: Each of the questions number 9 through 13 consists of three sets of names and building codes. In each question, the two names and building codes on the same line are supposed to be exactly the same.

If you find an error or errors on only *one* of the sets in the question, mark your answer A; any *two* of the sets in the question, mark your answer B; all *three* of the sets in the question, mark your answer C; *none* of the sets in the question, mark your answer D.

Column I
Duvivier, Anne P. - X52714
Dyrborg, Alfred - B4217
Dymnick, JoAnne - P482596

Column II
Duviver, Anne P. - X52714
Dyrborg, Alfred - B4267
Dymnick, JoAnne - P482596

In the above sample question, the first set of names and building codes is not exactly the same because the last names are spelled differently (Duvivier - Duviver). The second set of names and building codes is not exactly the same because the building codes are different (B4217 - B4267). The third set of names and building codes is exactly the same. Since there are mistakes in two of the sets of names and building codes, the answer to the sample question is B.

Now answer the questions on the following page using, the same procedure.

Column I	Column II	
9. Lautmann, Gerald G. - C2483 Lawlor, Michael - W44639 Lawrence, John J. - H1358	Lautmann, Gerald C. - C2483 Lawler, Michael - W44639 Lawrence, John J. - H1358	9.____
10. Mittmann, Howard - J4113 Mitchell, William T.- M75271 Milan, T. Thomas - Q67533	Mittmann, Howard - J4113 Mitchell, William T.- M75271 Milan, T. Thomas - Q67553	10.____
11. Quarles, Vincent - J34760 Quinn, Alan N. - S38813 Quinones, Peter W. - B87467	Quarles, Vincent - J34760 Quinn, Alan N. - S38813 Quinones, Peter W. - B87467	11.____
12. Daniels, Harold H. - A26554 Dantzler, Richard - C35780 Davidson, Martina - E62901	Daniels, Harold H - A26544 Dantzler, Richard - 035780 Davidson, Martin - E62901	12.____
13. Graham, Cecil J. - I20244 Granger, Deborah - T86211 Grant, Charles L. - G5788	Graham, Cecil J. - I20244 Granger, Deborah - T86211 Grant, Charles L. - G5788	13.____

KEY (CORRECT ANSWERS)

1.	D		8.	C
2.	C		9.	B
3.	A		10.	A
4.	B		11.	D
5.	A		12.	C
6.	D		13.	D
7.	B			

TEST 4

Questions 1-9

DIRECTIONS: In questions 1 to 10 there are five pairs of numbers or letters and numbers. Compare each pair and decide how many pairs are *EXACTLY ALIKE. PRINT THE LETTER OF THE CORRECT ANSWER IN THE SPACE AT THE RIGHT.*
   A. if only one pair is exactly alike
   B. if only two pairs are exactly alike
   C. if only three pairs are exactly alike
   D. if only four pairs are exactly alike
   E. if all five pairs are exactly alike

1. 73-F......F-73   FF-73. . . .FF-73   1.____
    F-7373....F-7373   373-FF...337-FF
    F-733.....337-F

2. 0-17158. . ..0-17158   0-71518 ... 0-71518   2.____
    0-11758....0-11758   0-15817... 0-15817
    0-51178....0-51178

3. 1A-7908....1A-7908   7A-8901....7A-8091   3.____
    7A-891......7A-891   1A-9078....1A-9708.
    9A-7018....9A-7081

4. 2V-6426....2V-6246   2N-6246....2N-6246   4.____
    2V-6426....2N-6426   2N-6624....2N-6624
    2V-6462....2V-6462

5. 3NY-56......3ny-65   5NY-356.....3NY-356   5.____
    6NY-3566....3ny-3566   5NY-6536....5NY-6536
    3NY-5663....5ny-3663

6. COB-065....COB-065   BCL-506....BCL-506   6.____
    LBC-650....LBC-650   DLB-560....DLB-560
    CDB-056....COB-065

7. 4KQ-9130....4KQ-9130   4KQ-9310....4KQ-9130   7.____
    4KQ-9031....4KQ-9031   4KQ-9301....4KQ-9301
    4KQ-9013....4KQ-9013

8. MK-89......MK-98   98-MK......89-MK   8.____
    MSK-998........MSK-998 MOSK.......MOKS
    SMK-899....SMK-899

9. 8MD-2104....SMD-2014   2MD-8140....2MD-8140   9.____
    814-MD......814-MD   4MD-8201. . . .4MD-8201
    MD-281......MD-481

10. 161-035. .. .161-035   150-316.... 150-316   10.____
    315-160....315-160   131-650....131-650
    165-301....165-301

KEY (CORRECT ANSWERS)

1.	B	6.	D
2.	E	7.	D
3.	B	8.	B
4.	C	9.	C
5.	A	10.	E

———

TEST 5

DIRECTIONS: Each question or incomplete statement is followed by several suggested answers or completions. Select the one that *BEST* answers the question or completes the statement. *PRINT THE LETTER OF THE CORRECT ANSWER IN THE SPACE AT THE RIGHT.*

Questions 1-5

DIRECTIONS: Questions 1 through 5, inclusive, consist of groups of four displays representing license identification plates. Examine each group of plates and determine the number of plates in each group which are identical. Mark your answer sheets as follows:

    If only two plates are identical, mark answer A.
    If only three plates are identical, mark answer B.
    If all four plates are identical, mark answer C.
    If the plates are all different, mark answer D

EXAMPLE

ABC123   BCD123   ABC123   BCD235

Since only two plates are identical, the first and the third, the correct answer is A.

1.	PBV839	PVB839	PVB839	PVB839	1.____
2.	WTX083	WTX083	WTX083	WTX083	2.____
3.	B73609	D73906	BD7396	BD7906	3.____
4.	AK7423	AK7423	AK1423	A81324	4.____
5.	583Y10	683Y10	583Y01	583Y10	5.____

Questions 6-10

DIRECTIONS: Questions 6 through 10 consist of groups of numbers and letters similar to those which might appear on license plates. Each group of numbers and letters will be called a license identification. Choose the license identification lettered A, B, C, or D that *EXACTLY* matches the license identification shown next to the question number.

SAMPLE
NY 1977
ABC-123

A.	NY 1976	B.	NY 1977	C.	NY 1977	D.	NY 1977
	ABC-123		ABC-132		CBA-123		ABC-123

The license identification given is NY 1977. The only choice
ABC-123.
that exactly matches it is the license identification next to the letter D. The correct answer is therefore D.

6.   NY 1976   6.____
       QLT-781

A.	NJ 1976	B.	NY 1975	C.	NY 1976	D.	NY 1977
	QLT-781		QLT-781		QLT-781		QLT-781

7.   FLA 1977   7.____
       2-7LT58J

A.	FLA 1977	B.	FLA 1977	C.	FLA 1977	D.	LA 1977
	2-7TL58J		2-7LTJ58		2-7LT58J		2-7LT58J

8.   NY 1975   8.____
       OQC383

A.	NY 1975	B.	NY 1975	C.	NY 1975	D.	NY 1977
	OQC383		OQC833		QCQ383		OCQ383

9.   MASS 1977   9.____
       B-8DK02

A.	MISS 1977	B.	MASS 1977	C.	MASS 1976	D.	MASS 1977
	B-8DK02		B-8DK02		B-8DK02		B-80KD2

10.   NY 1976   10.____
        ZV0586

A.	NY 1976	B.	NY 1977	C.	NY 1976	D.	NY 1976
	2V0586		ZV0586		ZV0586		ZU0586

KEY (CORRECT ANSWERS)

1.	B	6.	C
2.	C	7.	C
3.	D	8.	A
4.	A	9.	B
5.	A	10.	C

TEST 6

DIRECTIONS: Assume that each of the capital letters in the table below represents the name of an employee enrolled in the city employees' retirement system. The number directly beneath the letter represents the agency for which the employee works, and the small letter directly beneath represents the code for the employee's account.

Name of Employee	L	O	T	Q	A	M	R	N	C
Agency	3	4	5	9	8	7	2	1	6
Account Code	r	f	b	i	d	t	g	e	n

In each of the following questions 1 through 3, the agency code numbers and the account code letters in Columns 2 and 3 should correspond to the capital letters in Column 1 and should be in the same consecutive order. For each question, look at each column carefully and mark your answer as follows:

If there are one or more errors *in Column 2 only* , mark your answer A.

If there are one or more errors *in Column 3 only,* mark your answer B.

If there are one or more errors in Column 2 and one or more errors in Column 3, mark your answer C.

If there are *NO* errors in either column, mark your answer D.

The following sample question is given to help you understand the procedure.

Column I	Column 2	Column 3
TQLMOC	583746	birtfn

In Column 2, the second agency code number (corresponding to letter Q) should be "9", not "8". Column 3 is coded correctly to Column 1. Since there is an error only in Column 2, the correct answer is A.

	Column 1	Column 2	Column 3	
1.	Q L N R C A	9 3 1 2 6 8	i r e g n d	1.___
2.	N R M O T C	1 2 7 5 4 6	e g f t b n	2.___
3.	R C T A L M	2 6 5 8 3 7	g n d b r t	3.___

KEY (CORRECT ANSWERS)

1. D
2. C
3. B

NAME and NUMBER COMPARISONS

COMMENTARY

This test seeks to measure your ability and disposition to do a job carefully and accurately, your attention to exactness and preciseness of detail, your alertness and versatility in discerning similarities and differences between things, and your power in systematically handling written language symbols.

It is actually a test of your ability to do academic and/or clerical work, using the basic elements of verbal (qualitative) and mathematical (quantitative) learning - words and numbers.

EXAMINATION SECTION
TEST 1

DIRECTIONS: In each line across the page there are three names or numbers that are much alike. Compare the three names or numbers and decide which ones are exactly alike. *PRINT IN THE SPACE AT THE RIGHT THE LETTER:*
   A.   if all THREE names or numbers are exactly ALIKE
   B.   if only the FIRST and SECOND names or numbers are ALIKE
   C.   if only the FIRST and THIRD names or numbers are ALIKE
   D.   if only the SECOND and THIRD names or numbers are ALIKE
   E.   if ALL THREE names or numbers are DIFFERENT

1.   Davis Hazen   David Hozen   David Hazen   1._____

2.   Lois Appel   Lois Appel   Lois Apfel   2._____

3.   June Allan   Jane Allan   Jane Allan   3._____

4.   10235   10235   10235   4._____

5.   32614   32164   32614   5._____

TEST 2

1.   2395890   2395890   2395890   1._____

2.   1926341   1926347   1926314   2._____

3.   E. Owens McVey   E. Owen McVey   E. Owen McVay   3._____

4.   Emily Neal Rouse   Emily Neal Rowse   Emily Neal Rowse   4._____

5.   H. Merritt Audubon   H. Merriott Audubon H. Merritt Audubon   5._____

TEST 3

1. 6219354	6219354	6219354	1.____
2. 2312793	2312793	2312793	2.____
3. 1065407	1065407	1065047	3.____
4. Francis Ransdell	Frances Ramsdell	Francis Ramsdell	4.____
5. Cornelius Detwiler	Cornelius Detwiler	Cornelius Detwiler	5.____

TEST 4

1. 6452054	6452654	6542054	1.____
2. 8501268	8501268	8501286	2.____
3. Ella Burk Newham	Ella Burk Newnham	Elena Burk Newnham	3.____
4. Jno. K. Ravencroft	Jno. H. Ravencroft	Jno. H. Ravencoft	4.____
5. Martin Wills Pullen	Martin Wills Pulen	Martin Wills Pullen	5.____

TEST 5

1. 3457988	3457986	3457986	1.____
2. 4695682	4695862	4695682	2.____
3. Stricklund Kaneydy	Sticklund Kanedy	Stricklund Kanedy	3.____
4. Joy Harlor Witner	Joy Harloe Witner	Joy Harloe Witner	4.____
5. R.M.O. Uberroth	R.M.O. Uberroth	R.N.O. Uberroth	5.____

TEST 6

1.	1592514	1592574	1592574	1._____
2.	2010202	2010202	2010220	2._____
3.	6177396	6177936	6177396	3._____
4.	Drusilla S. Ridgeley	Drusilla S. Ridgeley	Drusilla S. Ridgeley	4._____
5.	Andrei I. Toumantzev	Andrei I. Tourmantzev	Andrei I. Toumantzov	5._____

TEST 7

1.	5261383	5261383	5261338	1._____
2.	8125690	8126690	8125609	2._____
3.	W.E. Johnston	W.E. Johnson	W.E. Johnson	3._____
4.	Vergil L. Muller	Vergil L. Muller	Vergil L. Muller	4._____
5.	Atherton R. Warde	Asheton R. Warde	Atherton P. Warde	5._____

TEST 8

1.	013469.5	023469.5	02346.95	1._____
2.	33376	333766	333766	2._____
3.	Ling-Temco-Vought	Ling-Tenco-Vought	Ling-Temco Vought	3._____
4.	Lorilard Corp.	Lorillard Corp.	Lorrilard Corp.	4._____
5.	American Agronomics Corporation	American Agronomics Corporation	American Agronomic Corporation	5._____

TEST 9

1. 436592864	436592864	436592864	1.____
2. 197765123	197755123	197755123	2.____
3. Dewaay, Cortvriendt International S.A.	Deway, Cortvriendt International S.A.	Deway, Corturiendt International S.A.	3.____
4. Crédit Lyonnais	Crèdit Lyonnais	Crèdit Lyonais	4.____
5. Algemene Bank Nederland N.V.	Algamene Bank Nederland N.V.	Algemene Bank Naderland N.V.	5.____

———

TEST 10

1. 00032572	0.0032572	00032522	1.____
2. 399745	399745	398745	2.____
3. Banca Privata Finanziaria S.p.A.	Banca Privata Finanzaria S.P.A.	Banca Privata Finanziaria S.P.A.	3.____
4. Eastman Dillon, Union Securities & Co.	Eastman Dillon, Union Securities Co.	Eastman Dillon, Union Securities & Co.	4.____
5. Arnhold and S. Bleichroeder, Inc.	Arnhold & S. Bleichroeder, Inc.	Arnold and S. Bleichroeder, Inc.	5.____

———

TEST 11

DIRECTIONS: Answer the questions below on the basis of the following instructions: For each such numbered set of names, addresses and numbers listed in Columns I and II, select your answer from the following options:

A: The names in Columns I and II are different
B: The addresses in Columns I and II are different
C: The numbers in Columns I and II are different
D: The names, addresses and numbers are identical

1.	Francis Jones 62 Stately Avenue 96-12446	Francis Jones 62 Stately Avenue 96-21446	1._____
2.	Julio Montez 19 Ponderosa Road 56-73161	Julio Montez 19 Ponderosa Road 56-71361	2._____
3.	Mary Mitchell 2314 Melbourne Drive 68-92172	Mary Mitchell 2314 Melbourne Drive 68-92172	3._____
4.	Harry Patterson 25 Dunne Street 14-33430	Harry Patterson 25 Dunne Street 14-34330	4._____
5.	Patrick Murphy 171 West Hosmer Street 93-81214	Patrick Murphy 171 West Hosmer Street 93-18214	5._____

TEST 12

1.	August Schultz 816 St. Clair Avenue 53-40149	August Schultz 816 St. Claire Avenue 53-40149	1._____
2.	George Taft 72 Runnymede Street 47-04033	George Taft 72 Runnymede Street 47-04023	2._____
3.	Angus Henderson 1418 Madison Street 81-76375	Angus Henderson 1418 Madison Street 81-76375	3._____
4.	Carolyn Mazur 12 Riven/lew Road 38-99615	Carolyn Mazur 12 Rivervane Road 38-99615	4._____
5.	Adele Russell 1725 Lansing Lane 72-91962	Adela Russell 1725 Lansing Lane 72-91962	5._____

TEST 13

DIRECTIONS: The following questions are based on the instructions given below. In each of the following questions, the 3-line name and address in Column I is the master-list entry, and the 3-line entry in Column II is the information to be checked against the master list.

> If there is one line that is *not* exactly alike, mark your answer A.
> If there are two lines *not* exactly alike, mark your answer B.
> If there are three lines *not* exactly alike, mark your answer C.
> If the lines *all are* exactly alike, mark your answer D.

1. Jerome A. Jackson
   1243 14th Avenue
   New York, N.Y. 10023

   Jerome A. Johnson
   1234 14th Avenue
   New York, N.Y. 10023

   1.____

2. Sophie Strachtheim
   33-28 Connecticut Ave.
   Far Rockaway, N.Y. 11697

   Sophie Strachtheim
   33-28 Connecticut Ave.
   Far Rockaway, N.Y. 11697

   2.____

3. Elisabeth NT. Gorrell
   256 Exchange St
   New York, N.Y. 10013

   Elizabeth NT. Gorrell
   256 Exchange St.
   New York, N.Y. 10013

   3.____

4. Maria J. Gonzalez
   7516 E. Sheepshead Rd.
   Brooklyn, N.Y. 11240

   Maria J. Gonzalez
   7516 N. Shepshead Rd.
   Brooklyn, N.Y. 11240

   4.____

5. Leslie B. Brautenweiler
   21-57A Seller Terr.
   Flushing, N.Y. 11367

   Leslie B. Brautenwieler
   21-75ASeilerTerr.
   Flushing, N.J. 11367

   5.____

KEYS (CORRECT ANSWERS)

TEST 1	TEST 2	TEST 3	TEST 4	TEST 5	TEST 6	TEST 7
1. E	1. A	1. A	1. E	1. D	1. D	1. B
2. B	2. E	2. A	2. B	2. C	2. B	2. E
3. D	3. E	3. B	3. E	3. E	3. C	3. D
4. A	4. D	4. E	4. E	4. D	4. A	4. A
5. C	5. C	5. A	5. C	5. B	5. E	5. E

TEST 8	TEST 9	TEST 10	TEST 11	TEST 12	TEST 13
1. E	1. A	1. E	1. C	1. B	1. B
2. D	2. D	2. B	2. C	2. C	2. D
3. E	3. E	3. E	3. D	3. D	3. B
4. E	4. E	4. C	4. C	4. B	4. A
5. B	5. E	5. E	5. C	5. A	5. C

NAME and NUMBER COMPARISONS

COMMENTARY

This test seeks to measure your ability and disposition to do a job carefully and accurately, your attention to exactness and preciseness of detail, your alertness and versatility in discerning similarities and differences between things, and your power in systematically handling written language symbols.

It is actually a test of your ability to do academic and/or clerical work, using the basic elements of verbal (qualitative) and mathematical (quantitative) learning – words and numbers.

EXAMINATION SECTION
TEST 1

Tests 1-2

DIRECTIONS: Questions 1 through 6 consist of sets of names and addresses. In each question, the name and address in Column II should be an exact copy of the name and address in Column I. *PRINT IN THE SPACE AT THE RIGHT THE LETTER:*

A.   if there is a mistake only in the name
B.   if there is a mistake only in the address
C.   if there is a mistake in both name and address
D.   if there is no mistake in either name or address

SAMPLE:

Michael Filbert   Michael Filbert
456 Reade Street   645 Reade Street
New York, N.Y. 10013   New York, N.Y. 10013

Since there is a mistake only in the address, the answer is B.

1.   Esta Wong   Esta Wang   1._____
     141 West 68 St.   141 West 68 St.
     New York, N.Y. 10023   New York, N.Y. 10023

2.   Dr. Alberto Grosso   Dr. Alberto Grosso   2._____
     3475 12th Avenue   3475 12th Avenue
     Brooklyn, N.Y. 11218   Brooklyn, N.Y. 11218

3.   Mrs. Ruth Bortlas   Ms. Ruth Bortlas   3._____
     482 Theresa Ct.   482 Theresa Ct.
     Far Rockaway, N.Y. 11691   Far Rockaway, N.Y. 11169

4.   Mr. and Mrs. Howard Fox   Mr. and Mrs. Howard Fox   4._____
     2301 Sedgwick Ave.   231 Sedgwick Ave.
     Bronx, N.Y. 10468   Bronx, N.Y. 10468

5.   Miss Marjorie Black   Miss Margorie Black   5._____
     223 East 23 Street   223 East 23 Street
     New York, N.Y. 10010   New York, N.Y. 10010

6. Michelle Herman
    806 Valley Rd.
    Old Tappan, N.J. 07675

Michelle Hermann
806 Valley Dr.
Old Tappan, N.J. 07675

6._____

———

KEY (CORRECT ANSWERS)

1. A
2. D
3. C
4. B
5. A
6. C

———

TEST 2

DIRECTIONS: Questions 1 through 6 consist of sets of names and addresses. In each question, the name and address in Column II should be an exact copy of the name and address in Column I. *PRINT IN THE SPACE AT THE RIGHT THE LETTER:*

    A. if there is a mistake only in the name
    B. if there is a mistake only in the address
    C. if there is a mistake in both name and address
    D. if there is no mistake in either name or address

1. Ms. Joan Kelly
    313 Franklin Ave.
    Brooklyn, N.Y. 11202

    Ms. Joan Kielly
    318 Franklin Ave.
    Brooklyn, N.Y. 11202

    1.____

2. Mrs. Eileen Engel
    47-24 86 Road
    Queens, N.Y. 11122

    Mrs. Ellen Engel
    47-24 86 Road
    Queens, N.Y. 11122

    2.____

3. Marcia Michaels
    213 E. 81 St.
    New York, N.Y. 10012

    Marcia Michaels
    213 E. 81 St.
    New York, N.Y. 10012

    3.____

4. Rev. Edward J. Smyth
    1401 Brandeis Street
    San Francisco, Calif. 96201

    Rev. Edward J. Smyth
    1401 Brandies Street
    San Francisco, Calif. 96201

    4.____

5. Alicia Rodriguez
    24-68 81 St.
    Elmhurst, N.Y. 11122

    Alicia Rodriquez
    2468 81 St.
    Elmhurst, N.Y. 11122

    5.____

6. Ernest Eisemann
    21 Columbia St.
    New York, N.Y. 10007

    Ernest Eisermann
    21 Columbia St.
    New York, N.Y. 10007

    6.____

KEY (CORRECT ANSWERS)

1. C
2. A
3. D
4. B
5. C
6. A

TEST 3

DIRECTIONS: Questions 1 through 8 consist of names, locations and telephone numbers. In each question, the name, location and number in Column II should be an exact copy of the name, location and number in Column I. *PRINT IN THE SPACE AT THE RIGHT THE LETTER:*
A. if there is a mistake in one line only
B. if there is a mistake in two lines only
C. if there is a mistake in three lines only
D. if there are no mistakes in any of the lines

1. Ruth Lang
    EAM Bldg., Room C101
    625-2000, ext. 765

    Ruth Lang
    EAM Bldg., Room C110
    625-2000, ext. 765   1._____

2. Anne Marie Ionozzi
    Investigations, Room 827
    576-4000, ext. 832

    Anna Marie Ionozzi
    Investigation, Room 827
    566-4000, ext. 832   2._____

3. Willard Jameson
    Fm C Bldg. Room 687
    454-3010

    Willard Jamieson
    Fm C Bldg. Room 687
    454-3010   3._____

4. Joanne Zimmermann
    Bldg. SW, Room 314
    532-4601

    Joanne Zimmermann
    Bldg. SW, Room 314
    532-4601   4._____

5. Carlyle Whetstone
    Payroll Division-A, Room 212A
    262-5000, ext. 471

    Caryle Whetstone
    Payroll Division-A, Room 212A
    262-5000, ext. 417   5._____

6. Kenneth Chiang
    Legal Council, Room 9745
    (201) 416-9100, ext. 17

    Kenneth Chiang
    Legal Counsel, Room 9745
    (201) 416-9100, ext. 17   6._____

7. Ethel Koenig
    Personnel Services Div, Rm 433
    635-7572

    Ethel Hoenig
    Personal Services Div, Rm 433
    635-7527   7._____

8. Joyce Ehrhardt
    Office of Administrator, Rm W56
    387-8706

    Joyce Ehrhart
    Office of Administrator, Rm W56
    387-7806   8._____

_____

KEY (CORRECT ANSWERS)

1. A
2. C
3. A
4. D
5. B

6. A
7. C
8. B

———

TEST 4

DIRECTIONS: Each of questions 1 through 10 gives the identification number and name of a person who has received treatment at a certain hospital. You are to choose the option (A, B, C or D) which has EXACTLY the same number and name as those given in the question.

SAMPLE:
123765 Frank Y. Jones
A. 123675 Frank Y. Jones
B. 123765 Frank T. Jones
C. 123765 Frank Y. Johns
D. 123765 Frank Y. Jones

The correct answer is D, because it is the only option showing the identification number and name exactly as they are in the sample question.

1. 754898 Diane Malloy   1.____

A. 745898 Diane Malloy
B. 754898 Dion Malloy
C. 754898 Diane Malloy
D. 754898 Diane Maloy

2. 661818 Ferdinand Figueroa   2.____

A. 661818 Ferdinand Figeuroa
B. 661618 Ferdinand Figueroa
C. 661818 Ferdnand Figueroa
D. 661818 Ferdinand Figueroa

3. 100101 Norman D. Braustein   3.____

A. 100101 Norman D. Braustein
B. 101001 Norman D. Braustein
C. 100101 Norman P. Braustien
D. 100101 Norman D. Bruastein

4. 838696 Robert Kittredge   4.____

A. 838969 Robert Kittredge
B. 838696 Robert Kittredge
C. 388696 Robert Kittredge
D. 838696 Robert Kittridge

5. 243716 Abraham Soletsky   5.____

A. 243716 Abrahm Soletsky
B. 243716 Abraham Solestky
C. 243176 Abraham Soletsky
D. 243716 Abraham Soletsky

6. 981121 Phillip M. Maas   6.____

     A. 981121 Phillip M. Mass
     B. 981211 Phillip M. Maas
     C. 981121 Phillip M. Maas
     D. 981121 Phillip N. Maas

7. 786556 George Macalusso   7.____

     A. 785656 George Macalusso
     B. 786556 George Macalusso
     C. 786556 George Maculusso
     D. 786556 George Macluasso

8. 639472 Eugene Weber   8.____

     A. 639472 Eugene Weber
     B. 639472 Eugene Webre
     C. 693472 Eugene Weber
     D. 639742 Eugene Weber

9. 724936 John J. Lomonaco   9.____

     A. 724936 John J. Lomanoco
     B. 724396 John L. Lomonaco
     C. 724936 John J. Lomonaco
     D. 724936 John J. Lamonaco

10. 899868 Michael Schnitzer   10.____

     A. 899868 Micheal Schnitzer
     B. 898968 Michael Schnizter
     C. 899688 Michael Schnitzer
     D. 899868 Michael Schnitzer

KEY (CORRECT ANSWERS)

1.	C	6.	C
2.	D	7.	B
3.	A	8.	A
4.	B	9.	C
5.	D	10.	D

CODING

COMMENTARY

An ingenious question-type called coding, involving elements of alphabetizing, filing, name and number comparison, and evaluative judgment and application, has currently won wide acceptance in testing circles for measuring clerical aptitude and general ability, particularly on the senior (middle) grades (levels).

While the directions for this question usually vary in detail, the candidate is generally asked to consider groups of names, codes, and numbers, and, then, according to a given plan, to arrange codes in alphabetic order; to arrange these in numerical sequence; to re-arrange columns of names and numbers in correct order; to espy errors in coding; to choose the correct coding arrangement in consonance with the given directions and examples, etc.

This question-type appears to have few paramaters in respect to form, substance, or degree of difficulty.

Accordingly, acquaintance with, and practice in, the coding question is recommended for the serious candidate.

EXAMINATION SECTION
TEST 1

DIRECTIONS:

CODE TABLE

Name of Applicant	H A N G S B R U K E
Test Code	c o m p l e x i t y
File Number	0 1 2 3 4 5 6 7 8 9

Assume that each of the above *capital letters* is the first letter of the Name of an Applicant, that the *small letter* directly beneath each capital letter is the Test Code for the Applicant, and that the *number* directly beneath each code letter is the File Number for the Applicant.
In each of the following questions, the test code letters and the file numbers in Columns 2 and 3 should correspond to the capital letters in Column 1. For each question, look at each column carefully and mark your answer as follows:

If there is an error only in Column 2, mark your answer A.
If there is an error only in Column 3, mark your answer B.
If there is an error in both Columns 2 and 3, mark your answer C.
If both Columns 2 and 3 are correct, mark your answer D.

The following sample question is given to help you understand the procedure.

SAMPLE QUESTION

Column 1	Column 2	Column 3
AKEHN	otyci	18902

In Column 2, the final test code letter "i" should be "m." Column 3 is correctly coded to Column 1. Since there is an error only in Column 2, the answer is A

	Column 1	Column 2	Column 3	
1.	NEKKU	mytti	29987	1.___
2.	KRAEB	txlye	86095	2.___
3.	ENAUK	ymoit	92178	3.___
4.	REANA	xeomo	69121	4.___
5.	EKHSE	ytcxy	97049	5.___

KEY (CORRECT ANSWERS)

1. B
2. C
3. D
4. A
5. C

TEST 2

DIRECTIONS: The employee identification codes in Column I begin and end with a capital letter and have an eight-digit number in between. In Questions 1 through 8, employee identification codes in Column I are to be arranged according to the following rules:

First: Arrange in alphabetical order according to the first letter.

Second: When two or more employee identification codes have the same first letter, arrange in alphabetical order according to the last letter.

Third: When two or more employee codes have the same first and last letters, arrange in numerical order beginning with the lowest number.

The employee identification codes in Column I are numbered 1 through 5 in the order in which they are listed. In Column II the numbers 1 through 5 are arranged in four different ways to show different arrangements of the corresponding employee identification numbers. Choose the answer in Column II in which the employee identification numbers are arranged according to the above rules.

SAMPLE QUESTION

Column I	Column II
1. E75044127B	A. 4, 1, 3, 2, 5
2. B96399104A	B. 4, 1, 2, 3, 5
3. B93939086A	C. 4, 3, 2, 5, 1
4. B47064465H	D. 3, 2, 5, 4, 1
5. B99040922A	

In the sample question, the four employee identification codes starting with B should be put before the employee identification code starting with E. The employee identification codes starting with B and ending with A should be put before the employee identification codes starting with B and ending with H. The three employee identification codes starting with B and ending with A should be listed in numerical order, beginning with the lowest number. The correct way to arrange the employee identification codes, therefore, is 3, 2, 5, 4, 1 shown below.

3.	B93939086A
2.	B96399104A
5.	B99040922A
4.	B47064465H
1.	E75044127B

Therefore, the answer to the sample question is D. Now answer the following questions according to the above rules.

	Column I		Column II	
1.	1. G42786441J		A. 2, 5, 4, 3, 1	1.____
	2. H45665413J		B. 5, 4, 1, 3, 2	
	3. G43117690J		C. 4, 5, 1, 3, 2	
	4. G435466981		D. 1, 3, 5, 4, 2	
	5. G416799421			

2.
1. S44556178T
2. T43457169T
3. S53321176T
4. T53317998S
5. S67673942S

A. 1, 3, 5, 2, 4
B. 4, 3, 5, 2, 1
C. 5, 3, 1, 2, 4
D. 5, 1, 3, 4, 2

2.____

3.
1. R63394217D
2. R63931247D
3. R53931247D
4. R66874239D
4. R46799366D

A. 5, 4, 2, 3, 1
B. 1, 5, 3, 2, 4
C. 5, 3, 1, 2, 4
D. 5, 1, 2, 3, 4

3.____

4.
1. A35671968B
2. A35421794C
3. A35466987B
4. C10435779A
5. C00634779B

A. 3, 2, 1, 4, 5
B. 2, 3, 1, 5, 4
C. 1, 3, 2, 4, 5
D. 3, 1, 2, 4, 5

4.____

5.
1. I99746426Q
2. I10445311Q
3. J63749877P
4. J03421739Q
5. J00765311Q

A. 2, 1, 3, 5, 4
B. 5, 4, 2, 1, 3
C. 4, 5, 3, 2, 1
D. 2, 1, 4, 5, 3

5.____

6.
1. M33964217N
2. N33942770N
3. N06155881M
4. M00433669M
5. M79034577N

A. 4, 1, 5, 2, 3
B. 5, 1, 4, 3, 2
C. 4, 1, 5, 3, 2
D. 1, 4, 5, 2, 3

6.____

7.
1. D77643905C
2. D44106788C
3. D13976022F
4. D97655430E
5. D00439776F

A. 1, 2, 5, 3, 4
B. 5, 3, 2, 1, 4
C. 2, 1, 5, 3, 4
D. 2, 1, 4, 5, 3

7.____

8.
1. W22746920A
2. W22743720A
3. W32987655A
4. W43298765A
5. W30987433A

A. 2, 1, 3, 4, 5
B. 2, 1, 5, 3, 4
C. 1, 2, 3, 4, 5
D. 1, 2, 5, 3, 4

8.____

KEY (CORRECT ANSWERS)

1.	B	5.	A
2.	D	6.	C
3.	C	7.	D
4.	D	8.	B

TEST 3

DIRECTIONS: Each of the following equestions consists of three sets of names and name codes. In each question, the two names and name codes on the same line are supposed to be exactly the same.

Look carefully at each set of names and codes and mark your answer:
- A. if there are mistakes in all three sets
- B. if there are mistakes in two of the sets
- C. if there is a mistake in only one set
- D. if there are no mistakes in any of the sets

The following sample question is given to help you understand the procedure.

Macabe, John N. - V 53162	Macade, John N. - V 53162
Howard, Joan S. - J 24791	Howard, Joan S. - J 24791
Ware, Susan B. - A 45068	Ware, Susan B. - A 45968

In the above sample question, the names and name codes of the first set are not exactly the same because of the spelling of the last name (Macabe - Macade). The names and name codes of the second set are exactly the same. The names and name codes of the third set are not exactly the same because the two name codes are different (A 45068 - A 45968), Since there are mistakes in only 2 of the sets, the answer to the sample question is B.

1. Powell, Michael C. - 78537 F   Powell, Michael C. - 78537 F   1.____
    Martinez, Pablo, J. - 24435 P   Martinez, Pablo J. - 24435 P
    MacBane, Eliot M. - 98674 E   MacBane, Eliot M. - 98674 E

2. Fitz-Kramer Machines Inc. - 259090   Fitz-Kramer Machines Inc. - 259090   2.____
    Marvel Cleaning Service - 482657   Marvel Cleaning Service - 482657
    Donate, Carl G. - 637418   Danato, Carl G. - 687418

3. Martin Davison Trading Corp. - 43108 T   Martin Davidson Trading Corp. - 43108 T   3.____
    Cotwald Lighting Fixtures - 76065 L   Cotwald Lighting Fixtures - 70056 L
    R. Crawford Plumbers - 23157 C   R. Crawford Plumbers - 23157 G

4. Fraiman Engineering Corp. - M4773   Friaman Engineering Corp. -M4773   4.____
    Neuman, Walter B. - N7745   Neumen, Walter B. - N7745
    Pierce, Eric M. - W6304   Pierce, Eric M. - W6304

5. Constable, Eugene - B 64837   Comstable, Eugene - B 64837   5.____
    Derrick, Paul - H 27119   Derrik, Paul - H 27119
    Heller, Karen - S 49606   Heller, Karen - S 46906

6. Hernando Delivery Service Co. - D 7456   Hernando Delivery Service Co. - D 7456   6.____
    Barettz Electrical Supplies - N 5392 Barettz Electrical Supplies - N 5392
    Tanner, Abraham - M 4798   Tanner, Abraham - M 4798

7. Kalin Associates - R 38641   Kaline Associates - R 38641   7.____
    Sealey, Robert E. - P 63533   Sealey, Robert E. - P 63553
    Scalsi Office Furniture   Scalsi Office Furniture

8. Janowsky, Philip M.- 742213
    Hansen, Thomas H. - 934816
    L. Lester and Son Inc. - 294568

Janowsky, Philip M.- 742213
Hanson, Thomas H. - 934816
L. Lester and Son Inc. - 294568

8.____

———

KEY (CORRECT ANSWERS)

1. D
2. C
3. A
4. B
5. A

6. D
7. B
8. C

———

TEST 4

DIRECTIONS: The following questions are to be answered on the basis of the following Code Table. In this table, for each number, a corresponding code letter is given. Each of the questions contains three pairs of numbers and code letters. In each pair, the code letters should correspond with the numbers in accordance with the Code Table.

CODE TABLE

Number	1	2	3	4	5	6	7	8	9	0
Corresponding Code Letter	Y	N	Z	X	W	T	U	P	S	R

In some of the pairs below, an error exists in the coding. Examine the pairs in each question carefully. If an error exists in:

Only one of the pairs in the question, mark your answer A.
Any two pairs in the question, mark your answer B.
All three pairs in the question, mark your answer C.
None of the pairs in the question, mark your answer D.

SAMPLE QUESTION

37258   -   ZUNWP
948764   -   SXPTTX
73196   -   UZYSP

In the above sample, the first pair is correct since each number, as listed, has the correct corresponding code letter. In the second pair, an error exists because the number 7 should have the code letter U instead of the letter T. In the third pair, an error exists because the number 6 should have the code letter T instead of the letter P. Since there are errors in two of the three pairs, the correct answer is B.

1. 493785   -   XSZUPW   1._____
    86398207   -   PTUSPNRU
    5943162   -   WSXZYTN

2. 5413968412   -   WXYZSTPXYR   2._____
    8763451297   -   PUTZXWYZSU
    4781965302   -   XUPYSUWZRN

3. 79137584   -   USYRUWPX   3._____
    638247   -   TZPNXS
    49679312   -   XSTUSZYN

4. 37854296   -   ZUPWXNST   4._____
    09183298   -   RSYXZNSP
    91762358   -   SYUTNXWP

5. 3918762485   -   ZSYPUTNXPW   5._____
    1578291436   -   YWUPNSYXZT
    2791385674   -   NUSYZPWTUX

6. 197546821 - YSUWSTPNY
    873024867 - PUZRNWPTU
    583179246 - WPZYURNXT

7. 510782463 - WYRUSNXTZ
    478192356 - XUPYSNZWT
    961728532 - STYUNPWXN

6.____

7.____

———

KEY (CORRECT ANSWERS)

1. A
2. C
3. B
4. B
5. D

6. C
7. B

———

TEST 5

DIRECTIONS: Assume that each of the capital letters is the first letter of the name of a city using EAM equipment. The number directly beneath each capital letter is the code number for the city. The small letter beneath each code number is the code letter for the number of EAM divisions in the city and the + or - symbol directly beneath each code letter is the code symbol which signifies whether or not the city uses third generation computers with the EAM equipment.

The questions that follow show City Letters in Column I, Code Numbers in Column II, Code Letters in Column III, and Code Symbols in Column IV. If correct. each City Letter in Column I should correspond by position with each of the three codes shown in the other three columns, in accordance with the coding key shown. *BUT* there are some errors. For each question,

If there is a total of *ONE* error in Columns 2, 3, and 4, mark your answer A.
If there is a total of *TWO* errors in Columns 2, 3, and 4, mark your answer B.
If there is a total of *THREE* errors in Columns 2, 3, and 4, mark your answer C.
If Columns 2, 3, and 4 are correct, mark your answer D.

SAMPLE QUESTION

I	II	III	IV
City Letter	Code Numbers	Code Letters	Code Symbols
Y J M O S	5 3 7 9 8	e b g i h	- - + + -

The errors are as follows: In Column 2, the Code Number should be "2" instead of "3" for City Letter "J," and in Column 4 the Code Symbol should be "+" instead of "-" for City Letter "Y." Since there is a total of two errors in Columns 2, 3, and 4, the answer to this sample question is B.

Now answer questions 1 through 9 according to these rules.

CODING KEY

City	Letter	P	J	R	T	Y	K	M	S	0
Code	Number	1	2	3	4	5	6	7	8	9
Code	Letter	a	b	c	d	e	f	g	h	i
Code	Symbol	+	-	+	-	+	-	+	-	+

	I	II	III	IV	
	City Letters	Code Numbers	Code Letters	Code Symbols	
1.	K O R M P	6 9 3 7 1	f i e g a	- - + + +	1.____
2.	O T P S Y	9 4 1 8 6	b d a h e	+ - - - +	2.____
3.	R S J T M	3 8 1 4 7	c h b e g	- - - - +	3.____
4.	P M S K J	1 7 8 6 2	a g h f b	+ + - - -	4.____
5.	M Y T J R	7 5 4 2 3	g e d f c	+ + - - +	5.____
6.	T P K Y O	4 1 6 7 9	d a f e i	- + - + -	6.____
7.	S K O R T	8 6 9 3 5	h f i c d	- - + + -	7.____
8.	J R Y P K	2 3 5 1 9	b d e a f	- + + + -	8.____
9.	R O M P Y	4 9 7 1 5	c i g a d	+ + - + +	9.____

KEY (CORRECT ANSWERS)

1. B
2. C
3. C
4. D
5. A

6. B
7. A
8. B
9. C

———

TEST 6

Assume that each of the capital letters is the first letter of the name of an offense, that the small letter directly beneath each capital letter is the code letter for the offense, and that the number directly beneath each code letter is the file number for the offense.

DIRECTIONS: In each of the following questions, the code letters and file numbers should correspond to the capital letters.

    If there is an error only in Column 2, mark your answer A.
    If there is an error only in Column 3, mark your answer B.
    If there is an error in both Column 2 and Column 3, mark your answer C.
    If both Columns 2 and 3 are correct, mark your answer D.

SAMPLE QUESTION

Column 1	Column 2	Column 3
BNARGHSVVU	emoxtylcci	6357905118

The code letters in Column 2 are correct but the first "5" in Column 3 should be "2." Therefore, the answer is B. Now answer the following questions according to the above rules.

CODE TABLE

Name of Offense	V A N D S B R U G H
Code Letter	c o m p l e x i t y
File Number	1 2 3 4 5 6 7 8 9 0

	Column 1	Column 2	Column 3	
1.	HGDSBNBSVR	ytplxmelcx	0945736517	1._____
2.	SDGUUNHVAH	lptiimycoy	5498830120	2._____
3.	BRSNAAVUDU	exlmooctpi	6753221848	3._____
4.	VSRUDNADUS	cleipmopil	1568432485	4._____
5.	NDSHVRBUAG	mplycxeiot	3450175829	5._____
6.	GHUSNVBRDA	tyilmcexpo	9085316742	6._____
7.	DBSHVURANG	pesycixomt	4650187239	7._____
8.	RHNNASBDGU	xymnolepti	7033256398	8._____

KEY (CORRECT ANSWERS)

1. C
2. D
3. A
4. C
5. B

6. D
7. A
8. C

———

TEST 7

DIRECTIONS: Each of the following questions contains three sets of code letters and code numbers. In each set, the code numbers should correspond with the code letters as given in the Table, but there is a coding error in some of the sets. Examine the sets in each question carefully.

Mark your answer A if there is a coding error in only *ONE* of the sets in the question.
Mark your answer B if there is a coding error in any *TWO* of the sets in the question.
Mark your answer C if there is a coding error in all *THREE* sets in the question.
Mark your answer D if there is a coding error in *NONE* of the sets in the question.

SAMPLE QUESTION

fgzduwaf - 35720843
uabsdgfw - 04262538
hhfaudgs - 99340257

In the above sample question, the first set is right because each code number matches the code letter as in the Code Table. In the second set, the corresponding number for the code letter b is wrong because it should be 1 instead of 2. In the third set, the corresponding number for the last code letter s is wrong because it should be 6 instead of 7. Since there is an error in two of the sets, the answer to the above sample question is B.

In the Code Table below, each code letter has a corresponding code number directly beneath it.

CODE TABLE

Code Letter	b	d	f	a	g	s	z	w	h	u
Code Number	1	2	3	4	5	6	7	8	9	0

1. fsbughwz - 36104987   zwubgasz - 78025467   1.____
    ghgufddb - 59583221

2. hafgdaas - 94351446   ddsfabsd - 22734162   2.____
    wgdbssgf - 85216553

3. abfbssbd - 41316712   ghzfaubs - 59734017   3.____
    sdbzfwza - 62173874

4. whfbdzag - 89412745   daaszuub - 24467001   4.____
    uzhfwssd - 07936623

5. zbadgbuh - 71425109   dzadbbsz - 27421167   5.____
    gazhwaff - 54798433

6. fbfuadsh - 31304265   gzfuwzsb - 57300671   6.____
    bashhgag - 14699535

KEY (CORRECT ANSWERS)

1. B
2. C
3. B
4. B
5. D
6. C

TEST 8

CODE TABLE

Letter	P	L	A	N	D	C	0	B	U	R
Corresponding Code Number	1	2	3	4	5	6	7	8	9	0

In some of the pairs below, an error exists in the coding. Examine the pairs in each question. Mark your answer

A if there is a mistake in only *one* of the pairs
B if there is a mistake in only *two* of the pairs
C if there is a mistake in *all three* of the pairs
D if there is a mistake in *none* of the pairs

SAMPLE QUESTION

LCBPUPAB -   26819138
ACOABOL   -   3683872
NDURONUC -   46901496

In the above sample, the first pair is correct since each letter as listed has the correct corresponding code number. In the second pair, an error exists because the letter 0 should have the code number 7, instead of 8. In the third pair, an error exists because the letter D should have the code number 5, instead of 6. Since there are errors in two of the three pairs, your answer should be B.

1. ADCANPLC - 35635126   DORURBBO - 57090877   1.____
   PNACBUCP - 14368061

2. LCOBLRAP - 26782931   UPANUPCD - 91349156   2.____
   RLDACLRO - 02536207

3. LCOROPAR - 26707130   BALANRUP - 83234091   3.____
   DOPOAULL - 57173922

4. ONCRUBAP - 74609831   DCLANORD - 56243705   4.____
   AORPDUR - 3771590

5. PANRBUCD - 13408965   UAOCDPLR - 93765120   5.____
   OPDDOBRA - 71556803

6. BAROLDCP - 83072561   PNOCOBLA - 14767823   6.____
   BURPDOLA - 89015723

7. ANNCPABO - 34461387   DBALDRCP - 58325061   7.____
   ACRPOUL - 3601792

119

8. BLAPOUR - 8321790   NOACNPL - 4736412   8.____
     RODACORD - 07536805

9. ADUBURCL- 3598062   NOCOBAPR - 47578310   9.____
     PRONDALU - 10754329

10. UBADCLOR - 98356270   NBUPPARA - 48911033   10.____
      LONDUPRC - 27459106

KEY (CORRECT ANSWERS)

1. C
2. B
3. D
4. B
5. A

6. D
7. B
8. B
9. C
10. A

TEST 9

DIRECTIONS: Answer questions 1 through 10 ONLY on the basis of the following information.
    Column I consists of serial numbers of dollar bills. Column II shows different ways of arranging the corresponding serial numbers.
    The serial numbers of dollar bills in Column I begin and end with a capital letter and have an eight-digit number in between. The serial numbers in Column I are to be arranged according to the following rules:

FIRST: In alphabetical order according to the first letter.

SECOND: When two or more serial numbers have the same first letter, in alphabetical order according to the last letter.

THIRD: When two or more serial numbers have the same first *and* last letters, in numerical order, beginning with the lowest number.

    The serial numbers in Column I are numbered (1) through (5) in the order in which they are listed. In Column II the numbers (1) through (5) are arranged in four different ways to show different arrangements of the corresponding serial numbers. Choose the answer in Column II in which the serial numbers are arranged according to the above rules.

SAMPLE QUESTION

	COLUMN I		COLUMN II
(1)	E75044127B	(A)	4, 1, 3, 2, 5
(2)	B96399104A	(B)	4, 1, 2, 3, 5
(3)	B93939086A	(C)	4, 3, 2, 5, 1
(4)	B47064465H	(D)	3, 2, 5, 4, 1
(5)	B99040922A		

    In the sample question, the four serial numbers starting with B should be put before the serial number starting with E. The serial numbers starting with B and ending with A should be put before the serial number starting with B and ending with H. The three serial numbers starting with B and ending with A should be listed in numerical order, beginning with the lowest number. The correct way to arrange the serial numbers, therefore, is:

(3)	B93939086A
(2)	B96399104A
(5)	B99040922A
(4)	B47064465H
(1)	E75044127B

Since the order of arrangement is 3, 2, 5, 4, 1, the answer to the sample question is (D).

		COLUMN I		COLUMN II
1.	(1)	P44343314Y	A.	2, 3, 1, 4, 5
	(2)	P44141341S	B.	1, 5, 3, 2, 4
	(3)	P44141431L	C.	4, 2, 3, 5, 1
	(4)	P41143413W	D.	5, 3, 2, 4, 1
	(5)	P44313433H		
2.	(1)	D89077275M	A.	3, 2, 5, 4, 1
	(2)	D98073724N	B.	1, 4, 3, 2, 5
	(3)	D90877274N	C.	4, 1, 5, 2, 3
	(4)	D98877275M	D.	1, 3, 2, 5, 4
	(5)	D98873725N		

			A.	2,	4,	5,	1,	3
3.	(1)	H32548137E	B.	1,	5,	2,	3,	4
	(2)	H35243178A	C.	1,	5,	2,	4,	3
	(3)	H35284378F	D.	2,	1,	5,	3,	4
	(4)	H35288337A						
	(5)	H32883173B						
4.	(1)	K24165039H	A.	4,	2,	5,	3,	1
	(2)	F24106599A	B.	2,	3,	4,	1,	5
	(3)	L21406639G	C.	4,	2,	5,	1,	3
	(4)	C24156093A	D.	1,	3,	4,	5,	2
	(5)	K24165593D						
5.	(1)	H79110642E	A.	2,	1,	3,	5,	4
	(2)	H79101928E	B.	2,	1,	4,	5,	3
	(3)	A79111567F	C.	3,	5,	2,	1,	4
	(4)	H79111796E	D.	4,	3,	5,	1,	2
	(5)	A79111618F						
6.	(1)	P16388385W	A.	3,	4,	5,	2,	1
	(2)	R16388335V	B.	2,	3,	4,	5,	1
	(3)	P16383835W	C.	2,	4,	3,	1,	5
	(4)	R18386865V	D.	3,	1,	5,	2,	4
	(5)	P18686865W						
7.	(1)	B42271749G	A.	4,	1,	5,	2,	3
	(2)	B42271779G	B.	4,	1,	2,	5,	3
	(3)	E43217779G	C.	1,	2,	4,	5,	3
	(4)	B42874119C	D.	5,	3,	1,	2,	4
	(5)	E42817749G						
8.	(1)	M57906455S	A.	4,	1,	5,	3,	2
	(2)	N87077758S	B.	3,	4,	1,	5,	2
	(3)	N87707757B	C.	4,	1,	5,	2,	3
	(4)	M57877759B	D.	1,	5,	3,	2,	4
	(5)	M57906555S						
9.	(1)	C69336894Y	A.	2,	5,	3,	1,	4
	(2)	C69336684V	B.	3,	2,	5,	1,	4
	(3)	C69366887W	C.	3,	1,	4,	5,	2
	(4)	C69366994Y	D.	2,	5,	1,	3,	4
	(5)	C69336865V						
10.	(1)	A56247181D	A.	1,	5,	3,	2,	4
	(2)	A56272128P	B.	3,	1,	5,	2,	4
	(3)	H56247128D	C.	3,	2,	1,	5,	4
	(4)	H56272288P	D.	1,	5,	2,	3,	4
	(5)	A56247188D						

KEY (CORRECT ANSWERS)

1.	D	6.	D
2.	B	7.	B
3.	A	8.	A
4.	C	9.	A
5.	C	10.	D

TEST 10

DIRECTIONS: Answer the following questions on the basis of the instructions, the code, and the sample questions given below. Assume that an officer at a certain location is equipped with a two-way radio to keep him in constant touch with his security headquarters. Radio messages and replies are given in code form, as follows:

CODE TABLE

Radio Code for Situation	J	P	M	F	B
Radio Code for Action to be Taken	o	r	a	z	q
Radio Response for Action Being Taken	1	2	3	4	5

Assume that each of the above capital letters is the radio code for a particular type of situation, that the small letter below each capital letter is the radio code for the action an officer is directed to take, and that the number directly below each small letter is the radio response an officer should make to indicate what action was actually taken.

In each of the following questions, the code letter for the action directed (Column 2) and the code number for the action taken (Column 3) should correspond to the capital letters in Column 1.

INSTRUCTIONS: If only Column 2 is different from Column 1, mark your answer I.
If only Column 3 is different from Column 1, mark your answer II.
If both Column 2 and Column 3 are different from Column I, mark your answer III.
If both Columns 2 and 3 are the same as Column 1, mark your answer IV.

SAMPLE QUESTION

Column 1	Column 2	Column 3
JPFMB	orzaq	12453

The CORRECT answer is: A. I B. II C. III D. IV
The code letters in Column 2 are correct, but the numbers "53" in Column 3 should be "35." Therefore, the answer is B. Now answe the following questions according to the above rules.

	Column 1	Column 2	Column 3	
1.	PBFJM	rqzoa	25413	1._____
2.	MPFBJ	zrqao	32541	2._____
3.	JBFPM	oqzra	15432	3._____
4.	BJPMF	qaroz	51234	4._____
5.	PJFMB	rozaq	21435	5._____
6.	FJBMP	zoqra	41532	6._____

KEY (CORRECT ANSWERS)

1.   D
2.   C
3.   B
4.   A
5.   D
6.   A

———

CLERICAL ABILITIES

EXAMINATION SECTION
TEST 1

DIRECTIONS: Each question or incomplete statement is followed by several suggested answers or completions. Select the one that BEST answers the question or completes the statement. *PRINT THE LETTER OF THE CORRECT ANSWER IN THE SPACE AT THE RIGHT.*

Questions 1-4.

DIRECTIONS: Questions 1 through 4 are to be answered on the basis of the information given below.

The most commonly used filing system and the one that is easiest to learn is alphabetical filing. This involves putting records in an A to Z order, according to the letters of the alphabet. The name of a person is filed by using the following order: first, the surname or last name; second, the first name; third, the middle name or middle initial. For example, *Henry C. Young* is filed under *Y* and thereafter under *Young, Henry C.* The name of a company is filed in the same way. For example, *Long Cabinet Co.* is filed under *L*, while *John T. Long Cabinet Co.* is filed under *L* and thereafter under *Long., John T. Cabinet Co.*

1. The one of the following which lists the names of persons in the CORRECT alphabetical order is:

   A. Mary Carrie, Helen Carrol, James Carson, John Carter
   B. James Carson, Mary Carrie, John Carter, Helen Carrol
   C. Helen Carrol, James Carson, John Carter, Mary Carrie
   D. John Carter, Helen Carrol, Mary Carrie, James Carson

1.____

2. The one of the following which lists the names of persons in the CORRECT alphabetical order is:

   A. Jones, John C.; Jones, John A.; Jones, John P.; Jones, John K.
   B. Jones, John P.; Jones, John K.; Jones, John C.; Jones, John A.
   C. Jones, John A.; Jones, John C.; Jones, John K.; Jones, John P.
   D. Jones, John K.; Jones, John C.; Jones, John A.; Jones, John P.

2.____

3. The one of the following which lists the names of the companies in the CORRECT alphabetical order is:

   A. Blane Co., Blake Co., Block Co., Blear Co.
   B. Blake Co., Blane Co., Blear Co., Block Co.
   C. Block Co., Blear Co., Blane Co., Blake Co.
   D. Blear Co., Blake Co., Blane Co., Block Co.

3.____

4. You are to return to the file an index card on *Barry C. Wayne Materials and Supplies Co.* Of the following, the CORRECT alphabetical group that you should return the index card to is

   A. A to G   B. H to M   C. N to S   D. T to Z

4.____

Questions 5-10.

DIRECTIONS: In each of Questions 5 through 10, the names of four people are given. For each question, choose as your answer the one of the four names given which should be filed FIRST according to the usual system of alphabetical filing of names, as described in the following paragraph.

In filing names, you must start with the last name. Names are filed in order of the first letter of the last name, then the second letter, etc. Therefore, BAILY would be filed before BROWN, which would be filed before COLT. A name with fewer letters of the same type comes first; i.e., Smith before Smithe. If the last names are the same, the names are filed alphabetically by the first name. If the first name is an initial, a name with an initial would come before a first name that starts with the same letter as the initial. Therefore, I. BROWN would come before IRA BROWN. Finally, if both last name and first name are the same, the name would be filed alphabetically by the middle name, once again an initial coming before a middle name which starts with the same letter as the initial. If there is no middle name at all, the name would come before those with middle initials or names.

Sample Question: A.   Lester Daniels
                            B.   William Dancer
                            C.   Nathan Danzig
                            D.   Dan Lester

The last names beginning with D are filed before the last name beginning with L. Since DANIELS, DANCER, and DANZIG all begin with the same three letters, you must look at the fourth letter of the last name to determine which name should be filed first. C comes before I or Z in the alphabet, so DANCER is filed before DANIELS or DANZIG. Therefore, the answer to the above sample question is B.

5.   A.   Scott Biala
     B.   Mary Byala
     C.   Martin Baylor
     D.   Francis Bauer
          5._____

6.   A.   Howard J. Black
     B.   Howard Black
     C.   J. Howard Black
     D.   John H. Black
          6._____

7.   A.   Theodora Garth Kingston
     B.   Theadore Barth Kingston
     C.   Thomas Kingston
     D.   Thomas T. Kingston
          7._____

8.   A.   Paulette Mary Huerta
     B.   Paul M. Huerta
     C.   Paulette L. Huerta
     D.   Peter A. Huerta
          8._____

9.   A.   Martha Hunt Morgan
     B.   Martin Hunt Morgan
     C.   Mary H. Morgan
     D.   Martine H. Morgan

9.____

10. A.   James T. Meerschaum
     B.   James M. Mershum
     C.   James F. Mearshaum
     D.   James N. Meshum

10.____

Questions 11-14.

DIRECTIONS: Questions 11 through 14 are to be answered SOLELY on the basis of the following information.

You are required to file various documents in file drawers which are labeled according to the following pattern:

DOCUMENTS

MEMOS		LETTERS	
File	Subject	File	Subject
84PM1	(A-L)	84PC1	(A-L)
84PM2	(M-Z)	84PC2	(M-Z)

REPORTS		INQUIRIES	
File	Subject	File	Subject
84PR1	(A-L)	84PQ1	(A-L)
84PR2	(M-Z)	84PQ2	(M-Z)

11.   A letter dealing with a burglary should be filed in the drawer labeled

   A.   84PM1   B.   84PC1   C.   84PR1   D.   84PQ2

11.____

12.   A report on Statistics should be found in the drawer labeled

   A.   84PM1   B.   84PC2   C.   84PR2   D.   84PQ2

12.____

13.   An inquiry is received about parade permit procedures. It should be filed in the drawer labeled

   A.   84PM2   B.   84PC1   C.   84PR1   D.   84PQ2

13.____

14.   A police officer has a question about a robbery report you filed.
      You should pull this file from the drawer labeled

   A.   84PM1   B.   84PM2   C.   84PR1   D.   84PR2

14.____

Questions 15-22.

DIRECTIONS: Each of Questions 15 through 22 consists of four or six numbered names. For each question, choose the option (A, B, C, or D) which indicates the order in which the names should be filed in accordance with the following filing instructions:
   - File alphabetically according to last name, then first name, then middle initial.
   - File according to each successive letter within a name.

- When comparing two names in which, the letters in the longer name are identical to the corresponding letters in the shorter name, the shorter name is filed first.
- When the last names are the same, initials are always filed before names beginning with the same letter.

15.
    I.   Ralph Robinson
    II.   Alfred Ross
    III. Luis Robles
    IV. James Roberts

The CORRECT filing sequence for the above names should be

A. IV, II, I, III
C. III, IV, I, II

B. I, IV, III, II
D. IV, I, III, II

15.___

16.
    I.   Irwin Goodwin
    II.   Inez Gonzalez
    III. Irene Goodman
    IV. Ira S. Goodwin
    V.   Ruth I. Goldstein
    VI. M.B. Goodman

The CORRECT filing sequence for the above names should be

A. V, II, I, IV, III, VI
C. V, II, III, VI, IV, I

B. V, II, VI, III, IV, I
D. V, II, III, VI, I, IV

16.___

17.
    I.   George Allan
    II.   Gregory Allen
    III. Gary Allen
    IV. George Allen

The CORRECT filing sequence for the above names should be

A. IV, III, I, II
C. III, IV, I, II

B. I, IV, II, III
D. I, III, IV, II

17.___

18.
    I.   Simon Kauffman
    II.   Leo Kaufman
    III. Robert Kaufmann
    IV. Paul Kauffmann

The CORRECT filing sequence for the above names should be

A. I, IV, II, III
C. III, II, IV, I

B. II, IV, III, I
D. I, II, III, IV

18.___

19.
    I.   Roberta Williams
    II.   Robin Wilson
    III. Roberta Wilson
    IV. Robin Williams

The CORRECT filing sequence for the above names should be

A. III, II, IV, I
C. I, II, III, IV

B. I, IV, III, II
D. III, I, II, IV

19.___

20.
I. Lawrence Shultz
II. Albert Schultz
III. Theodore Schwartz
IV. Thomas Schwarz
V. Alvin Schultz
VI. Leonard Shultz

20.____

The CORRECT filing sequence for the above names should be

A. II, V, III, IV, I, VI
C. II, V, I, VI, III, IV
B. IV, III, V, I, II, VI
D. I, VI, II, V, III, IV

21.
I. McArdle
II. Mayer
III. Maletz
IV. McNiff
V. Meyer
VI. MacMahon

21.____

The CORRECT filing sequence for the above names should be

A. I, IV, VI, III, II, V
C. VI, III, II, I, IV, V
B. II, I, IV, VI, III, V
D. VI, III, II, V, I, IV

22.
I. Jack E. Johnson
II. R.H. Jackson
III. Bertha Jackson
IV. J.T. Johnson
V. Ann Johns
VI. John Jacobs

22.____

The CORRECT filing sequence for the above names should be

A. II, III, VI, V, IV, I
C. VI, II, III, I, V, IV
B. III, II, VI, V, IV, I
D. III, II, VI, IV, V, I

Questions 23-30.

DIRECTIONS: The code table below shows 10 letters with matching numbers. For each question, there are three sets of letters. Each set of letters is followed by a set of numbers which may or may not match their correct letter according to the code table. For each question, check all three sets of letters and numbers and mark your answer:

    A. if no pairs are correctly matched
    B. if only one pair is correctly matched
    C. if only two pairs are correctly matched
    D. if all three pairs are correctly matched

CODE TABLE

T	M	V	D	S	P	R	G	B	H
1	2	3	4	5	6	7	8	9	0

Sample Question: TMVDSP - 123456
                       RGBHTM - 789011
                       DSPRGB - 256789

In the sample question above, the first set of numbers correctly matches its set of letters. But the second and third pairs contain mistakes. In the second pair, M is incorrectly matched with number 1. According to the code table, letter M should be correctly matched with number 2. In the third pair, the letter D is incorrectly matched with number 2. According to the code table, letter D should be correctly matched with number 4. Since only one of the pairs is correctly matched, the answer to this sample question is B.

23.   RSBMRM 759262   23.____
      GDSRVH 845730
      VDBRTM 349713

24.   TGVSDR 183247   24.____
      SMHRDP 520647
      TRMHSR 172057

25.   DSPRGM 456782   25.____
      MVDBHT 234902
      HPMDBT 062491

26.   BVPTRD 936184   26.____
      GDPHMB 807029
      GMRHMV 827032

27.   MGVRSH 283750   27.____
      TRDMBS 174295
      SPRMGV 567283

28.   SGBSDM 489542   28.____
      MGHPTM 290612
      MPBMHT 269301

29.   TDPBHM 146902   29.____
      VPBMRS 369275
      GDMBHM 842902

30.   MVPTBV 236194   30.____
      PDRTMB 647128
      BGTMSM 981232

KEY (CORRECT ANSWERS)

1.	A	11.	B	21.	C
2.	C	12.	C	22.	B
3.	B	13.	D	23.	B
4.	D	14.	D	24.	B
5.	D	15.	D	25.	C
6.	B	16.	C	26.	A
7.	B	17.	D	27.	D
8.	B	18.	A	28.	A
9.	A	19.	B	29.	D
10.	C	20.	A	30.	A

TEST 2

DIRECTIONS: Each question or incomplete statement is followed by several suggested answers or completions. Select the one that BEST answers the question or completes the statement. *PRINT THE LETTER OF THE CORRECT ANSWER IN THE SPACE AT THE RIGHT.*

Questions 1-10.

DIRECTIONS: Questions 1 through 10 each consists of two columns, each containing four lines of names, numbers and/or addresses. For each question, compare the lines in Column I with the lines in Column II to see if they match exactly, and mark your answer A, B, C, or D, according to the following instructions:
- A. all four lines match exactly
- B. only three lines match exactly
- C. only two lines match exactly
- D. only one line matches exactly

		COLUMN I	COLUMN II	
1.	I.	Earl Hodgson	Earl Hodgson	1.____
	II.	1409870	1408970	
	III.	Shore Ave.	Schore Ave.	
	IV.	Macon Rd.	Macon Rd.	
2.	I.	9671485	9671485	2.____
	II.	470 Astor Court	470 Astor Court	
	III.	Halprin, Phillip	Halperin, Phillip	
	IV.	Frank D. Poliseo	Frank D. Poliseo	
3.	I.	Tandem Associates	Tandom Associates	3.____
	II.	144-17 Northern Blvd.	144-17 Northern Blvd.	
	III.	Alberta Forchi	Albert Forchi	
	IV.	Kings Park, NY 10751	Kings Point, NY 10751	
4.	I.	Bertha C. McCormack	Bertha C. McCormack	4.____
	II.	Clayton, MO.	Clayton, MO.	
	III.	976-4242	976-4242	
	IV.	New City, NY 10951	New City, NY 10951	
5.	I.	George C. Morill	George C. Morrill	5.____
	II.	Columbia, SC 29201	Columbia, SD 29201	
	III.	Louis Ingham	Louis Ingham	
	IV.	3406 Forest Ave.	3406 Forest Ave.	
6.	I.	506 S. Elliott Pl.	506 S. Elliott Pl.	6.____
	II.	Herbert Hall	Hurbert Hall	
	III.	4712 Rockaway Pkway	4712 Rockaway Pkway	
	IV.	169 E. 7 St.	169 E. 7 St.	

	COLUMN I	COLUMN II	
7.	I. 345 Park Ave.	345 Park Pl.	7.____
	II. Colman Oven Corp.	Coleman Oven Corp.	
	III. Robert Conte	Robert Conti	
	IV. 6179846	6179846	
8.	I. Grigori Schierber	Grigori Schierber	8.____
	II. Des Moines, Iowa	Des Moines, Iowa	
	III. Gouverneur Hospital	Gouverneur Hospital	
	IV. 91-35 Cresskill Pl.	91-35 Cresskill Pl.	
9.	I. Jeffery Janssen	Jeffrey Janssen	9.____
	II. 8041071	8041071	
	III. 40 Rockefeller Plaza	40 Rockafeller Plaza	
	IV. 407 6 St.	406 7 St.	
10.	I. 5971996	5871996	10.____
	II. 3113 Knickerbocker Ave.	3113 Knickerbocker Ave.	
	III. 8434 Boston Post Rd.	8424 Boston Post Rd.	
	IV. Penn Station	Penn Station	

Questions 11-14.

DIRECTIONS: Questions 11 through 14 are to be answered by looking at the four groups of names and addresses listed below (I, II, III, and IV) and then finding out the number of groups that have their corresponding numbered lines exactly the same.

GROUP I
Line 1. Richmond General Hospital
Line 2. Geriatric Clinic
Line 3. 3975 Paerdegat St.
Line 4 Loudonville, New York 11538

GROUP II
Richman General Hospital
Geriatric Clinic
3975 Peardegat St.
Londonville, New York 11538

GROUP III
Line 1. Richmond General Hospital
Line 2. Geriatric Clinic
Line 3. 3795 Paerdegat St.
Line 4. Loudonville, New York 11358

GROUP IV
Richmend General Hospital
Geriatric Clinic
3975 Paerdegat St.
Loudonville, New York 11538

11. In how many groups is line one exactly the same?　　　　　　　　　　　11.____

    A. Two   B. Three   C. Four   D. None

12. In how many groups is line two exactly the same?　　　　　　　　　　　12.____

    A. Two   B. Three   C. Four   D. None

13. In how many groups is line three exactly the same?　　　　　　　　　　13.____

    A. Two   B. Three   C. Four   D. None

14. In how many groups is line four exactly the same?　14.____

　　A. Two　　　　B. Three　　　C. Four　　　D. None

Questions 15-18.

DIRECTIONS: Each of Questions 15 through 18 has two lists of names and addresses. Each list contains three sets of names and addresses. Check each of the three sets in the list on the right to see if they are the same as the corresponding set in the list on the left. Mark your answers:
　　A. if none of the sets in the right list are the same as those in the left list
　　B. if only one of the sets in the right list is the same as those in the left list
　　C. if only two of the sets in the right list are the same as those in the left list
　　D. if all three sets in the right list are the same as those in the left list

15.　　Mary T. Berlinger
　　　2351 Hampton St.
　　　Monsey, N.Y. 20117

　　　Eduardo Benes
　　　473 Kingston Avenue
　　　Central Islip, N.Y. 11734

　　　Alan Carrington Fuchs
　　　17 Gnarled Hollow Road
　　　Los Angeles, CA 91635

　　　Mary T. Berlinger
　　　2351 Hampton St.
　　　Monsey, N.Y. 20117

　　　Eduardo Benes
　　　473 Kingston Avenue
　　　Central Islip, N.Y. 11734

　　　Alan Carrington Fuchs
　　　17 Gnarled Hollow Road
　　　Los Angeles, CA 91685　　15.____

16.　　David John Jacobson
　　　178 35 St. Apt. 4C
　　　New York, N.Y. 00927

　　　Ann-Marie Calonella
　　　7243 South Ridge Blvd.
　　　Bakersfield, CA 96714

　　　Pauline M. Thompson
　　　872 Linden Ave.
　　　Houston, Texas 70321

　　　David John Jacobson
　　　178 53 St. Apt. 4C
　　　New York, N.Y. 00927

　　　Ann-Marie Calonella
　　　7243 South Ridge Blvd.
　　　Bakersfield, CA 96714

　　　Pauline M. Thomson
　　　872 Linden Ave.
　　　Houston, Texas 70321　　16.____

17.　　Chester LeRoy Masterton
　　　152 Lacy Rd.
　　　Kankakee, Ill. 54532

　　　William Maloney
　　　S. LaCrosse Pla.
　　　Wausau, Wisconsin 52146

　　　Cynthia V. Barnes
　　　16 Pines Rd.
　　　Greenpoint, Miss. 20376

　　　Chester LeRoy Masterson
　　　152 Lacy Rd.
　　　Kankakee, Ill. 54532

　　　William Maloney
　　　S. LaCross Pla.
　　　Wausau, Wisconsin 52146

　　　Cynthia V. Barnes
　　　16 Pines Rd.
　　　Greenpoint, Miss. 20376　　17.____

18.   Marcel Jean Frontenac   Marcel Jean Frontenac   18._____
       8 Burton On The Water   6 Burton On The Water
       Calender, Me. 01471   Calender, Me. 01471

       J. Scott Marsden   J. Scott Marsden
       174 S. Tipton St.   174 Tipton St.
       Cleveland, Ohio   Cleveland, Ohio

       Lawrence T. Haney   Lawrence T. Haney
       171 McDonough St.   171 McDonough St.
       Decatur, Ga. 31304   Decatur, Ga. 31304

Questions 19-26.

DIRECTIONS: Each of Questions 19 through 26 has two lists of numbers. Each list contains
              three sets of numbers. Check each of the three sets in the list on the right to
              see if they are the same as the corresponding set in the list on the left. Mark
              your answers:
              A.   if none of the sets in the right list are the same as those in the left list
              B.   if only one of the sets in the right list is the same as those in the left
                   list
              C.   if only two of the sets in the right list are the same as those in the left
                   list
              D.   if all three sets in the right list are the same as those in the left list

19.   7354183476   7354983476   19._____
       4474747744   4474747774
       57914302311   57914302311

20.   7143592185   7143892185   20._____
       8344517699   8344518699
       9178531263   9178531263

21.   2572114731   257214731   21._____
       8806835476   8806835476
       8255831246   8255831246

22.   331476853821   331476858621   22._____
       6976658532996   6976655832996
       3766042113715   3766042113745

23.   8806663315   8806663315   23._____
       74477138449   74477138449
       211756663666   211756663666

24.   990006966996   99000696996   24._____
       53022219743   53022219843
       4171171117717   4171171177717

25.   24400222433004   24400222433004   25._____
       5300030055000355   5300030055500355
       20000075532002022   20000075532002022

26. 611166640660001116   61116664066001116   26._____
     711130011700110073   71113001170011000733
     26666446664476518   26666446664476518

Questions 27-30.

DIRECTIONS: Questions 27 through 30 are to be answered by picking the answer which is in
              the correct numerical order, from the lowest number to the highest number, in
              each question.

27.   A. 44533, 44518, 44516, 44547   27._____
      B. 44516, 44518, 44533, 44547
      C. 44547, 44533, 44518, 44516
      D. 44518, 44516, 44547, 44533

28.   A. 95587, 95593, 95601, 95620   28._____
      B. 95601, 95620, 95587, 95593
      C. 95593, 95587, 95601, 95620
      D. 95620, 95601, 95593, 95587

29.   A. 232212, 232208, 232232, 232223   29._____
      B. 232208, 232223, 232212, 232232
      C. 232208, 232212, 232223, 232232
      D. 232223, 232232, 232208, 232212

30.   A. 113419, 113521, 113462, 113588   30._____
      B. 113588, 113462, 113521, 113419
      C. 113521, 113588, 113419, 113462
      D. 113419, 113462, 113521, 113588

KEY (CORRECT ANSWERS)

1.	C	11.	A	21.	C
2.	B	12.	C	22.	A
3.	D	13.	A	23.	D
4.	A	14.	A	24.	A
5.	C	15.	C	25.	C
6.	B	16.	B	26.	C
7.	D	17.	B	27.	B
8.	A	18.	B	28.	A
9.	D	19.	B	29.	C
10.	C	20.	B	30.	D

Memory for Addresses

DESCRIPTION OF THE TEST AND SAMPLE QUESTIONS

All Clerks in the Post Office have to learn a scheme during their training period. The Clerk uses the scheme to sort the mail to where it is going. He must have a good memory in order to learn the scheme. Carriers also need good memories.

In this test you will be given 25 addresses to remember. The addresses are divided into five groups. Each group of five addresses is in a box such as those below. Each box has a letter—A, B, C, D, or E. You will have to learn which letter goes with each address. You will be given time to study in the examination room. In order to practice for this test, you need to be timed.

While you are doing the practice test, find out what is the best way for you to memorize which letter goes with each address. Some people learn best by studying the addresses in one box; then covering it and seeing whether they can say the addresses to themselves. If they can say them, they then try to learn the next box. If they cannot, they study the names in the first box again; and then try to say the names with the box covered. They do this for all the boxes. Other people learn best by studying across the page. Still others do best by memorizing everything at once. If you do not know your best way, try different ways and see which one is best for you. Do not try to memorize the names by writing them down because you won't be allowed to write them in the official examination.

Hints for Memory for Addresses Test

- Be sure to spend the study period studying.
- Be sure to try to learn which letter goes with each address. It is to your advantage to learn as many as you can.
- Do not spend too much time on any one question.
- Do not get nervous about the time limit. (In the official test no one is expected to do all the questions in the time allowed.)
- If you are not sure of an answer, guess.

2

Sample Questions for Memory for Addresses

In this test you will have five boxes labeled A, B, C, D, and E. Each box contains five addresses. Three of the five are groups of street addresses like 1700–2599 Wood, 8500–8699 Lang, and 6200–6399 James, and two are names of places. They are different in each box.

You will also be given two lists of names. You will have to decide which box each name belongs in. When you are working on the first list, you will have the boxes with the names in front of you. When you are working on the second list, you will not be able to look at the boxes.

The addresses you will use for the Practice Test are given in the boxes below.

A	B	C	D	E
1700–2599 Wood Dushore 8500–8699 Lang Lott 6200–6399 James	2700–3299 Wood Jeriel 8700–9399 Lang Vanna 5700–6199 James	1300–1699 Wood Levering 9400–9499 Lang Ekron 6400–6499 James	3300–3599 Wood Bair 8000–8499 Lang Viborg 5000–5699 James	2600–2699 Wood Danby 9500–9999 Lang Lycan 4700–4999 James

Questions 1 through 5 show the way the questions look. You have to decide in which lettered box (A, B, C, D, or E) the address belongs and then mark that answer on the Sample Answer Sheet on this page.

1. Levering

   This address is in box C. So darken box C on the Sample Answer Sheet.

2. 2700–3299 Wood

   This address is in box B. So darken box B on the Sample Answer Sheet.

3. Vanna

   This address is in box B. So darken box B on the Sample Answer Sheet.

Now, you do questions 4 and 5.

4. 6200–6399 James

5. Bair

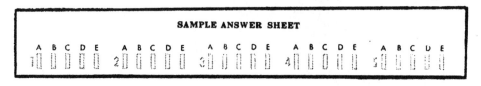

The answers for samples 4 and 5 are 4A and 5D.

Your practice test starts on the next page.

MEMORY FOR ADDRESSES---PRACTICE TEST

STUDY---*3 minutes*

Now turn back to page **2** and spend 3 minutes memorizing the addresses in the boxes. TRY TO LEARN THE LOCATION OF AS MANY ADDRESSES AS YOU CAN. Cover each box with your hand and see if you can repeat, to yourself, the addresses in that box.

When the 3 minutes for studying are up, turn to page **4** and continue with the practice.

4

List 1

WORK—*3 minutes*

For each question, mark the Sample Answer Sheet on the next page to show the letter of the box in which the address belongs. Try to remember the location of as many addresses as you can. If you are not sure of an address, guess. Work only 3 minutes.

A	B	C	D	E
1700–2599 Wood Dushore 8500–8699 Lang Lott 6200–6399 James	2700–3299 Wood Jeriel 8700–9399 Lang Vanna 5700–6199 James	1300–1699 Wood Levering 9400–9499 Lang Ekron 6400–6499 James	3300–3599 Wood Bair 8000–8499 Lang Viborg 5000–5699 James	2600–2699 Wood Danby 9500–9999 Lang Lycan 4700–4999 James

1. 6200–6399 James
2. 1700–2599 Wood
3. Bair
4. 1700–2599 Wood
5. Ekron
6. Viborg
7. Danby
8. 8500–8699 Lang

9. Lycan
10. 8000–8499 Lang
11. 4700–4999 James
12. 9400–9499 Lang
13. 2700–3299 Wood
14. Jeriel
15. 9500–9999 Lang
16. 1300–1699 Wood

17. 8700–9399 Lang
18. Levering
19. Vanna
20. 6400–6499 James
21. 3300–3599 Wood
22. Dushore
23. Lycan
24. 5700–6199 James

25. Lott
26. Viborg
27. Jeriel
28. 5000–5699 James
29. 2600–2699 Wood
30. 4700–4999 James
31. 2700–3299 Wood
32. 8000–8499 Lang

33. Ekron
34. 3300–3599 Wood
35. 9400–9499 Lang
36. 6200–6399 James
37. 2600–2699 Wood
38. 8500–8699 Lang
39. Levering
40. Lott

41. Bair
42. 1700–2599 Wood
43. 6400–6499 James
44. 9500–9999 Lang
45. Jeriel
46. 4700–4999 James
47. Dushore
48. Lycan

49. 1700–2599 Wood
50. 6200–6399 James
51. Vanna
52. Ekron
53. 8700–9399 Lang
54. Bair
55. 2600–2699 Wood
56. Dushore

57. 5700–6199 James
58. 1300–1699 Wood
59. Levering
60. Lott
61. Jeriel
62. 2600–2699 Wood
63. Lott
64. 4700–4999 James

65. Dushore
66. Danby
67. 8500–8699 Lang
68. Vanna
69. 2700–3299 Wood
70. 9500–9999 Lang
71. Viborg
72. Ekron

73. 6200–6399 James
74. 2600–2699 Wood
75. Levering
76. Lott
77. 1300–1699 Wood
78. Bair
79. Lycan
80. 5700–6199 James

81. Levering
82. 8700–9399 Lang
83. 5000–5699 James
84. 1700–2599 Wood
85. Jeriel
86. 6200–6399 James
87. Ekron
88. 2700–3299 Wood

STOP.

If you finish before the 3 minutes are up, go back and check your answers for the questions on this page for the rest of the 3 minutes.

When the 3 minutes are up, go on to page 6.

5

SAMPLE ANSWER SHEET

	A B C D E	A B C D E	A B C D E	A B C D E	A B C D E	A B C D E	A B C D E	A B C D E	A B C D E
	1 □□□□□	2 □□□□□	3 □□□□□	4 □□□□□	5 □□□□□	6 □□□□□	7 □□□□□	8 □□□□□	
	9 □□□□□	10 □□□□□	11 □□□□□	12 □□□□□	13 □□□□□	14 □□□□□	15 □□□□□	16 □□□□□	
	17 □□□□□	18 □□□□□	19 □□□□□	20 □□□□□	21 □□□□□	22 □□□□□	23 □□□□□	24 □□□□□	
	25 □□□□□	26 □□□□□	27 □□□□□	28 □□□□□	29 □□□□□	30 □□□□□	31 □□□□□	32 □□□□□	
	33 □□□□□	34 □□□□□	35 □□□□□	36 □□□□□	37 □□□□□	38 □□□□□	39 □□□□□	40 □□□□□	
	41 □□□□□	42 □□□□□	43 □□□□□	44 □□□□□	45 □□□□□	46 □□□□□	47 □□□□□	48 □□□□□	
	49 □□□□□	50 □□□□□	51 □□□□□	52 □□□□□	53 □□□□□	54 □□□□□	55 □□□□□	56 □□□□□	
	57 □□□□□	58 □□□□□	59 □□□□□	60 □□□□□	61 □□□□□	62 □□□□□	63 □□□□□	64 □□□□□	
	65 □□□□□	66 □□□□□	67 □□□□□	68 □□□□□	69 □□□□□	70 □□□□□	71 □□□□□	72 □□□□□	
	73 □□□□□	74 □□□□□	75 □□□□□	76 □□□□□	77 □□□□□	78 □□□□□	79 □□□□□	80 □□□□□	
	81 □□□□□	82 □□□□□	83 □□□□□	84 □□□□□	85 □□□□□	86 □□□□□	87 □□□□□	88 □□□□□	

List 2

WORK—*3 minutes*

Now do these questions without looking back at the boxes with the addresses in them.

For each question, mark your answer on the Sample Answer Sheet on the next page. If you are not sure of an answer, guess.

1. Jeriel	25. 2700–3299 Wood	49. Bair	73. Dushore
2. Dushore	26. 5700–6199 James	50. 8700–9399 Lang	74. 8000–8499 Lang
3. 5000–5699 James	27. Levering	51. 6200–6399 James	75. Bair
4. 1300–1699 Wood	28. 9500–9999 Lang	52. 9400–9499 Lang	76. Ekron
5. 8500–8699 Lang	29. 2600–2699 Wood	53. Viborg	77. 6200–6399 James
6. Bair	30. 3300–3599 Wood	54. 8000–8499 Lang	78. 3300–3599 Wood
7. 5700–6199 James	31. Viborg	55. 4700–4999 James	79. 8700–9399 Lang
8. Levering	32. 9400–9499 Lang	56. Lycan	80. Viborg
9. Danby	33. Jeriel	57. Vanna	81. 4700–4999 James
10. Viborg	34. Bair	58. Danby	82. Lycan
11. 8000–8499 Lang	35. 8500–8699 Lang	59. 5700–6199 James	83. 1700–2599 Wood
12. 2700–3299 Wood	36. 1700–2599 Wood	60. Lott	84. 8500–8699 Lang
13. 9400–9499 Lang	37. 8000–8499 Lang	61. 2700–3299 Wood	85. 1300–1699 Wood
14. 3300–3599 Wood	38. Danby	62. 5000–5699 James	86. Jeriel
15. 4700–4999 James	39. Ekron	63. 1700–2599 Wood	87. Danby
16. 9500–9999 Lang	40. 4700–4999 James	64. 8000–8499 Lang	88. 6400–6499 James
17. Ekron	41. Dushore	65. 9400–9499 Lang	
18. 1300–1699 Wood	42. Vanna	66. Jeriel	**STOP.**
19. Vanna	43. 5000–5699 James	67. 9500–9999 Lang	
20. Lycan	44. Lott	68. Dushore	If you finish before the
21. 8700–9399 Lang	45. 1300–1699 Wood	69. 2600–2699 Wood	end of 3 minutes, go back
22. Dushore	46. Levering	70. 8500–8699 Lang	and be sure that you
23. 6200–6399 James	47. 5700–6199 James	71. Levering	are satisfied with your
24. Lott	48. 9500–9999 Lang	72. 5000–5699 James	answers.

Second Study

STUDY—*5 minutes*

You can see that memory is important in this test.

Now turn back to page 2 and spend 5 minutes memorizing the addresses in the boxes. TRY TO MEMORIZE THE LOCATION OF AS MANY ADDRESSES AS YOU CAN. Cover each box with your hand and see if you can repeat, to yourself, the addresses in that box.

When the 5 minutes for studying are up, turn to page 8 and continue with the practice.

SAMPLE ANSWER SHEET

List 1—Second Time

WORK—5 minutes

For each question, mark your answer on the Sample Answer Sheet on the next page. Try to remember the location of as many addresses as you can.

A	B	C	D	E
1700–2599 Wood Dushore 8500–8699 Lang Lott 6200–6399 James	2700–3299 Wood Jeriel 8700–9399 Lang Vanna 5700–6199 James	1300–1699 Wood Levering 9400–9499 Lang Ekron 6400–6499 James	3300–3599 Wood Bair 8000–8499 Lang Viborg 5000–5699 James	2600–2699 Wood Danby 9500–9999 Lang Lycan 4700–4999 James

1. 6200–6399 James
2. 1700–2599 Wood
3. Bair
4. 1700–2599 Wood
5. Ekron
6. Viborg
7. Danby
8. 8500–8699 Lang

9. Lycan
10. 8000–8499 Lang
11. 4700–4999 James
12. 9400–9499 Lang
13. 2700–3299 Wood
14. Jeriel
15. 9500–9999 Lang
16. 1300–1699 Wood

17. 8700–9399 Lang
18. Levering
19. Vanna
20. 6400–6499 James
21. 3300–3599 Wood
22. Dushore
23. Lycan
24. 5700–6199 James

25. Lott
26. Viborg
27. Jeriel
28. 5000–5699 James
29. 2600–2699 Wood
30. 4700–4999 James
31. 2700–3299 Wood
32. 8000–8499 Lang

33. Ekron
34. 3300–3599 Wood
35. 9400–9499 Lang
36. 6200–6399 James
37. 2600–2699 Wood
38. 8500–8699 Lang
39. Levering
40. Lott

41. Bair
42. 1700–2599 Wood
43. 6400–6499 James
44. 9500–9999 Lang
45. Jeriel
46. 4700–4999 James
47. Dushore
48. Lycan

49. 1700–2599 Wood
50. 6200–6399 James
51. Vanna
52. Ekron
53. 8700–9399 Lang
54. Bair
55. 2600–2699 Wood
56. Dushore

57. 5700–6199 James
58. 1300–1699 Wood
59. Levering
60. Lott
61. Jeriel
62. 2600–2699 Wood
63. Lott
64. 4700–4999 James

65. Dushore
66. Danby
67. 8500–8699 Lang
68. Vanna
69. 2700–3299 Wood
70. 9500–9999 Lang
71. Viborg
72. Ekron

73. 6200–6399 James
74. 2600–2699 Wood
75. Levering
76. Lott
77. 1300–1699 Wood
78. Bair
79. Lycan
80. 5700–6199 James

81. Levering
82. 8700–9399 Lang
83. 5000–5699 James
84. 1700–2599 Wood
85. Jeriel
86. 6200–6399 James
87. Ekron
88. 2700–3299 Wood

STOP.

If you finish before the 5 minutes are up, go back and check your answers for the questions on this page.

At the end of 5 minutes, turn to page 10.

9

SAMPLE ANSWER SHEET

10

List 2—Second Time

List 2—Second Time

WORK—*5 minutes*

This is the section that counts. The other times were to help you learn the addresses.

Do these questions without looking back at the boxes with the addresses in them. Work for 5 minutes.

For each question, mark the Sample Answer Sheet on the next page to show the letter of the box in which the address belongs.

1. Jeriel
2. Dushore
3. 5000–5699 James
4. 1300–1699 Wood
5. 8500–8699 Lang
6. Bair
7. 5700–6199 James
8. Levering

9. Danby
10. Viborg
11. 8000–8499 Lang
12. 2700–3299 Wood
13. 9400–9499 Lang
14. 3300–3599 Wood
15. 4700–4999 James
16. 9500–9999 Lang

17. Ekron
18. 1300–1699 Wood
19. Vanna
20. Lycan
21. 8700–9399 Lang
22. Dushore
23. 6200–6399 James
24. Lott

25. 2700–3299 Wood
26. 5700–6199 James
27. Levering
28. 9500–9999 Lang
29. 2600–2699 Wood
30. 3300–3599 Wood
31. Viborg
32. 9400–9499 Lang

33. Jeriel
34. Bair
35. 8500–8699 Lang
36. 1700–2599 Wood
37. 8000–8499 Lang
38. Danby
39. Ekron
40. 4700–4999 James

41. Dushore
42. Vanna
43. 5000–5699 James
44. Lott
45. 1300–1699 Wood
46. Levering
47. 5700–6199 James
48. 9500–9999 Lang

49. Bair
50. 8700–9399 Lang
51. 6200–6399 James
52. 9400–9499 Lang
53. Viborg
54. 8000–8499 Lang
55. 4700–4999 James
56. Lycan

57. Vanna
58. Danby
59. 5700–6199 James
60. Lott
61. 2700–3299 Wood
62. 5000–5699 James
63. 1700–2599 Wood
64. 8000–8499 Lang

65. 9400–9499 Lang
66. Jeriel
67. 9500–9999 Lang
68. Dushore
69. 2600–2699 Wood
70. 8500–8699 Lang
71. Levering
72. 5000–5699 James

73. Dushore
74. 8000–8499 Lang
75. Bair
76. Ekron
77. 6200–6399 James
78. 3300–3599 Wood
79. 8700–9399 Lang
80. Viborg

81. 4700–4999 James
82. Lycan
83. 1700–2599 Wood
84. 8500–8699 Lang
85. 1300–1699 Wood
86. Jeriel
87. Danby
88. 6400–6499 James

STOP.

If you finish before the 5 minutes are up, go back and check your answers.

At the end of the 5 minutes, compare your answers with those given in the Correct Answers for sample questions on page 11.

SAMPLE ANSWER SHEET

Now check your answers by comparing your answers with the correct answers shown below.

CORRECT ANSWERS

Count how many you got right, and write that number on this line ⟶ Number Right _____

Now count how many you got wrong, and write that number on this line ⟶ Number Wrong _____

Divide the Number Wrong by 4, and write the answer on this line ⟶ ¼ Number Wrong _____

Subtract the ¼ Number Wrong from the Number Right, and write the Difference on this line ⟶ Total Score _____

(The meaning of your Test Score will be found on page 12.)

Meaning of Test Score

If your Total Score is *44 or more*, you have a Good score.

If your Total Score is from *26 to 43*, you have a Fair score.

If your Total Score is *25 or less*, you are not doing too well.

You may be going too slowly, or you may be making too many mistakes. You need more practice.

———

DOCUMENTS AND FORMS
PREPARING WRITTEN MATERIAL
EXAMINATION SECTION
TEST 1

DIRECTIONS: Each question or incomplete statement is followed by several suggested answers or completions. Select the one that BEST answers the question or completes the statement. *PRINT THE LETTER OF THE CORRECT ANSWER IN THE SPACE AT THE RIGHT.*

1.   Suppose that one of the forms you fill out daily requires some information which you know is unnecessary.
   Which is the BEST action to take?   1._____
     A. Refuse to supply the information you think is unnecessary.
     B. Continue to fill out the form as required, even though the information is unnecessary.
     C. Suggest to your supervisor that the form be revised to reflect useful information.
     D. Suggest that fewer copies of the form be required.

2.   Of the following, the MOST likely reason for recommending that your department establish a standard form for recording certain information would be that this information   2._____
     A. will be produced at some disciplinary hearing
     B. concerns a secret or confidential record about an unusual incident at the garage
     C. contains a detailed explanation of a complex procedure
     D. must be taken from a large number of people on a regular basis

3.   If the four steps listed below for processing records were given in logical sequence, the one that would be the THIRD step is   3._____
     A. coding the records, using a chart or classification system
     B. inspecting the records to make sure they have been released for filing
     C. preparing cross-reference sheets or cards
     D. skimming the records to determine filing captions

4.   Which of the following BEST describes "office work simplification"?   4._____
     A. An attempt to increase the rate of production by speeding up the movements of employees
     B. Eliminating wasteful steps in order to increase efficiency
     C. Making jobs as easy as possible for employees so they will not be overworked
     D. Eliminating all difficult tasks from an office and leaving only simple ones

5. The use of the same method of recordkeeping and reporting by all sections is   5.____
    A. *desirable*, mainly because it saves time in section operations
    B. *undesirable*, mainly because it kills the initiative of the individual section foreman
    C. *desirable*, mainly because it will be easier for the superior to evaluate and compare section operations
    D. *undesirable*, mainly because operations vary from section to section and uniform recordkeeping and reporting is not appropriate

6. The GREATEST benefit the section officer will have from keeping complete   6.____
and accurate records of section operations is that
    A. he will find it easier to run his section efficiently
    B. he will need less equipment
    C. he will need less manpower
    D. the section will run smoothly when he is out

7. You have prepared a report to your superior and are ready to send it forward.   7.____
But on reading it, you think some parts are not clearly expressed and the
superior may have difficulty getting your point.
Of the following, it would be BEST for you to
    A. give the report to one of your men to read, and, if he has no trouble understanding it, send it through
    B. forward the report and call the superior the next day to ask if it was all right
    C. forward the report as is; higher echelons should be able to understand any report prepared by a section officer
    D. do the report over, re-writing the sections you are doubtful of

8. Of the following, a flow chart is BEST described as a chart which shows   8.____
    A. the places through which work moves in the course of the job process
    B. which employees perform specific functions leading to the completion of a job
    C. the schedules for production and how they eliminate waiting time between jobs
    D. how work units are affected by the actions of related work units

9. A superior decided to hold a problem-solving conference with his entire staff   9.____
and distributed an announcement and agenda one week before the meeting.
Of the following, the BEST reason for providing each participate with an
agenda is that
    A. participants will feel that something will be accomplished
    B. participants may prepare for the conference
    C. controversy will be reduced
    D. the top man should state the expected conclusions

10. The one of the following activities which is generally the LEAST proper   10.____
function of a centralized procedures section is
   A. issuing new and revised procedural instructions
   B. coordinating forms revision and procedural changes
   C. accepting or rejecting authorized procedural changes
   D. controlling standard numbering systems for procedural releases

11. Assume that it is the policy of an operating unit to act on all requests   11.____
received within five working days. Several operations are involved in acting on
these requests. Each operation is performed by a separate sub-unit. The staff
of the unit is reasonable adequate to handle this workload.
If only one of the following can be done, the MOST effective procedure for
maintaining adherence to the unit's five-day processing policy is to
   A. maintain a central "tickler" file in each sub-unit for the requests received
daily in that sub-unit
   B. prepare a "tickler" card for each request and follow it up five days later to
determine whether action has been taken
   C. rely on standards of production for each operation as an incentive to the
employees of each sub-unit to meet the schedule
   D. schedule the operations on a timetable basis so that the request will be
forwarded from one sub-unit to another within specified time limits

12. When one or two simple changes are needed in a memo to another unit or   12.____
in a letter to a citizen, a unit head follows the practice of making such simple
changes neatly in ink.
This practice is GENERALLY
   A. *poor*, chiefly because it reflects unfavorably on the originating unit's ability
to make a decision
   B. *good*, chiefly because the department's public image is likely to be
improved when people see it as trying to save money and speed up its
processes
   C. *poor*, chiefly because a letter or document prepared in final form
represents an investment of department time and effort and should go out
only as a perfect finished product
   D. *good*, chiefly because the document may be important, and sending it
back for retyping may delay it too long to achieve its purpose

13. Suppose that one of the office machines in your unit is badly in need of   13.____
replacement.
Of the following, the MOST important reason for postponing immediate
purchase of a new machine would be that
   A. a later model of the machine is expected on the market in a few months
   B. the new machine is more expensive than the old machine
   C. the operator of the present machine will have to be instructed by the
manufacturer in the operation of the new machine
   D. the employee operating the old machine is not complaining

14. To avoid cutting off parts of letters when using an automatic letter opener, it is BEST to
    A. arrange all of the letters so that the addresses are right side up
    B. hold the envelopes up to the light to make sure their contents have not settled to the side that is to be opened
    C. strike the envelopes against a table or desktop several times so that the contents of all the envelopes settle to one side
    D. check the enclosures periodically to make sure that the machine has not been cutting into them

14.____

15. Of the following, the BEST reason for setting up a partitioned work area for the typists in our office is that
    A. an uninterrupted flow of work among the typists will be possible
    B. complaints about ventilation and lighting will be reduced
    C. the first-line supervisor will have more direct control over the typists
    D. the noise of the typewriters will be less disturbing to other workers

15.____

16. From the viewpoint of use of a typewriter to fill in a form, the MOST important design factor to consider is
    A. standard spacing   B. box headings
    C. serial numbering   D. vertical guide lines

16.____

17. Requests to repair office equipment which appears to be unsafe should be given priority MAINLY because, if repairs are delayed,
    A. there may be injuries to staff
    B. there may be further deterioration of the equipment
    C. work flow may be interrupted
    D. the cost of repair may increase

17.____

18. A clerk is asked to complete two assignments – transcribe a handwritten business letter and create a spreadsheet. Which two computer programs would the clerk use?
    A. Microsoft Word and Microsoft Excel
    B. Microsoft Word and Microsoft PowerPoint
    C. Google Docs and Google Chrome
    D. Adobe Reader and Microsoft PowerPoint

18.____

19. Generally, the actual floor space occupied by a standard letter-size office file cabinet, when closed, is MOST NEARLY
    A. ½ square foot   B. 3 square feet
    C. 7 square feet   D. 11 square feet

19.____

20. Suppose a clerk under your supervision accidentally opens a personal letter while handling office mail.
Under such circumstances, you should tell the clerk to put the letter back into the envelope and
    A. take the letter to the person to whom it belongs and make sure he understands that the clerk did not read it
    B. try to seal the envelope so it won't appear to have been opened

20.____

C. write on the envelope "Sorry – opened by mistake," and put his initials on it

D. write on the envelope "Sorry – opened by mistake," but not put his initials on it

21. Standard forms frequently call for entries on them to be printed. 21.____
The MAIN reason for this practice is that printing, as compared to writing, is GENERALLY
A. more compact
B. more legal
C. more legible
D. easier to do

22. After a stenographer types a letter which has been dictated, the finished 22.____
letter should be carefully read for errors.
If he dictator follows the procedure of carefully reading each transcribed letter, a stenographer, under your supervision, should, unless you instruct her otherwise
A. not take time to proofread transcribed letters
B. continue to carefully proofread transcribed letters
C. review transcribed letters for meaning rather than for errors in typing or transcription
D. review transcribed letters for errors in typing rather than for errors in transcription

23. In transcribing a letter, the secretary notes that the dictator said, "The series 23.____
of conferences are planned to be relevant to today's problems." In such a case, the secretary should
A. type the sentence as it appears in the notes
B. check with the dictator to see whether he would prefer a different grammatical construction
C. change the noun so that it is correct
D. revise the sentence as much as necessary to make it read better

24. Of the following, the BEST procedure for your staff to follow in transcribing 24.____
several letters that were dictated is to
A. transcribe first the letters that are most difficult so that they can return immediately to the dictator with any questions
B. read through the notes for each letter to be sure they have all the information needed before preparing the transcript
C. transcribe first those letters that are shortest and simplest in order to get them out of the way
D. read all the notes aloud to a co-worker to see whether they sound right

25. In typing long letters, which of the following is generally considered the 25.____
LEAST desirable practice?
A. Numbering the second and succeeding pages of the letter
B. Typing a single line of a new paragraph as the last line of a page
C. Dividing a word at the end of a line of typing
D. Typing the name of the recipient of the letter on the second and succeeding pages

───────────

KEY (CORRECT ANSWERS)

1.	C		11.	D
2.	D		12.	B
3.	D		13.	A
4.	B		14.	C
5.	C		15.	D
6.	A		16.	A
7.	D		17.	A
8.	A		18.	A
9.	B		19.	B
10.	C		20.	C

21.	C
22.	B
23.	B
24.	B
25.	B

TEST 2

DIRECTIONS: Each question or incomplete statement is followed by several suggested answers or completions. Select the one that BEST answers the question or completes the statement. *PRINT THE LETTER OF THE CORRECT ANSWER IN THE SPACE AT THE RIGHT.*

1. The use of a microfilm system for information storage and retrieval would make the MOST sense in an office where
   A. a great number of documents must be kept available for permanent reference
   B. documents are ordinarily kept on file for less than six months
   C. filing is a minor and unimportant part of the office work
   D. most of the records on file are working forms on which additional entries are frequently made

1.____

2. Of the following concepts, the one which CANNOT be represented suitably by a pie chart is
   A. percent shares
   B. shares in absolute units
   C. time trends
   D. successive totals over time, with their shares

2.____

3. A pictogram is ESSENTIALLY another version of a(n) _____ chart.
   A. plain bar
   B. component bar
   C. pie
   D. area

3.____

4. A time series for a certain cost is presented in a graph. It is drawn so that the vertical (cost) axis starts at a point well above zero. This is a legitimate method of presentation for some purposes, but it may have the effect of
   A. hiding fixed components of the cost
   B. exaggerating changes which, in actual amounts, may be insignificant
   C. minimizing variable components of the cost
   D. impairing correlation analysis

4.____

5. Certain budgetary data may be represented by bar, area, or volume charts. Which one of the following BEST expressed the most appropriate order of usefulness?
   A. Descends from bar to volume and area charts, the last two being about the same
   B. Descends from volume to area, to bar charts
   C. Depends on the nature of the data presented
   D. Descends from bar to area to volume charts

5.____

6. One weekend, you develop a painful infection in one hand. You know that your typing speed will be much slower than normal and the likelihood of your making mistakes will be increased.
Of the following, the BEST course of action for you to take in this situation is to
   A. report to work as scheduled and do your typing assignments as best you can without complaining
   B. report to work as scheduled and ask your co-workers to divide your typing assignments until your hand heals
   C. report to work as scheduled and ask your supervisor for non-typing assignments until your hand heals
   D. call in sick and remain on medical leave until your hand is completely healed so that you can perform your normal duties

6.____

7. When filling out a departmental form during an interview concerning a citizen complaint, an interviewer should know the purpose of each question that he asks the citizen. For such information to be supplied by your department is
   A. *advisable*, because the interviewer may lose interest in the job if he is not fully informed about the questions he has to ask
   B. *inadvisable*, because the interviewer may reveal the true purpose of the questions to the citizens
   C. *advisable*, because the interviewer might otherwise record superficial or inadequate answers if he does not fully understand the questions
   D. *inadvisable*, because the information obtained through the form may be of little importance to the interviewer

7.____

8. The one of the following which is the BEST reason for placing the date and time of receipt on incoming mail is that this procedure
   A. aids the filing of correspondence in alphabetical order
   B. fixes responsibility for promptness in answering correspondence
   C. indicates that the mail has been checked for the presence of a return address
   D. makes it easier to distribute the main in sequence

8.____

9. Which one of the following is the FIRST step that you should take when filing a document by subject?
   A. Arrange related documents by date with the latest date in front
   B. Check whether the document has been released for filing
   C. Cross-reference the document if necessary
   D. Determine the category under which the document will be filed

9.____

10. The one of the following which is NOT generally employed to keep track of frequently used material requiring future attention is a
   A. card tickler file   B. dated follow-up folder
   C. periodic transferal of records   D. signal folder

10.____

11. Which one of the following is NOT a useful filing practice?   11.____
   A. Filing active records in the most accessible parts of the file cabinet
   B. Filing a file drawer to capacity in order to save space
   C. Gluing small documents to standard-size paper before filing
   D. Using different colored labels for various filing categories

12. The one of the following cases in which you would NOT place a special   12.____
   notation in the left margin of a letter that you have typed is when
   A. one of the copies is intended for someone other than the addressee of
      the letter
   B. you enclose a flyer with the letter
   C. you sign your superior's name to the letter, at his or her request
   D. the letter refers to something being sent under separate cover

13. Suppose that you accidentally cut a letter or enclosure as you are opening   13.____
   an envelope with a paper knife. The one of the following that you should do
   FIRST is to
   A. determine whether the document is important
   B. clip or staple the pieces together and process as usual
   C. mend the cut document with transparent tape
   D. notify the sender that the communication was damaged and request
      another copy

14. It is generally advisable to leave at least six inches of working space in a   14.____
   file drawer. This procedure is MOST useful in
   A. decreasing the number of filing errors
   B. facilitating the sorting of documents and folders
   C. maintaining a regular program of removing inactive records
   D. preventing folders and papers from being torn

15. Of the following, the MOST important reason to sort large volumes of   15.____
   documents before filing is that sorting
   A. decreases the need for cross-referencing
   B. eliminates the need to keep the filing up-to-date
   C. prevents overcrowding of the file drawers
   D. saves time and energy in filing

16. When typing a preliminary draft of a report, the one of the following which   16.____
   you should generally NOT do is to
   A. erase typing errors and deletions rather than "X"ing them out
   B. leave plenty of room at the top, bottom, and sides of each page
   C. make only the number of copies that you are asked to make
   D. type double or triple space

17. When printing a 500-page office manual, the most efficient method is to use which of the following office machines?

    A. Inkjet printer
    B. Copy machine
    C. Word processor
    D. All-in-one scanner/fax/copier

17.____

18. When typing name or titles on a roll of folder labels, the one of the following which it is MOST important to do is to type the caption

    A. as it appears son the papers to be placed in the folder
    B. in capital letters
    C. in exact indexing or filing order
    D. so that it appears near the bottom of the folder tab when the label is attached

18.____

19. The MOST important reason for having color cartridges on hand for an office copier even though most prints are black and white is because

    A. color ink is used for all copies
    B. some copiers or printers will not print black and white if any of the color cartridges are empty
    C. black ink is cheaper when purchasing along with color cartridges
    D. lack of color ink can cause copier malfunctions

19.____

20. All of the following pertain to the formatting of word-processing documents EXCEPT

    A. headers and footers
    B. rows and columns
    C. indents and page breaks
    D. alignment and justified type

20.____

KEY (CORRECT ANSWERS)

1.	A	11.	B
2.	C	12.	C
3.	A	13.	C
4.	B	14.	D
5.	D	15.	D
6.	C	16.	A
7.	C	17.	B
8.	B	18.	C
9.	B	19.	B
10.	C	20.	B

SAMPLE QUESTIONS

BIOGRAPHICAL INVENTORY

The questions included in the Biographical Inventory ask for information about you and your background. These kinds of questions are often asked during an oral interview. For years, employers have been using interviews to relate personal history, preferences, and attitudes to job success. This Biographical Inventory attempts to do the same and includes questions which have been shown to be related to job success. It has been found that successful employees tend to select some answers more often than other answers, while less successful employees tend to select different answers. The questions in the Biographical Inventory do not have a single correct answer. Every choice is given some credit. More credit is given for answers selected more often by successful employees.

These Biographical Inventory questions are presented for illustrative purposes only. The answers have not been linked to the answers of successful employees; therefore, we cannot designate any "correct" answer(s).

DIRECTIONS: You may only mark ONE response to each question. It is possible that none of the answers applies well to you. However, one of the answers will surely be true (or less inaccurate) for you than others. In such a case, mark that answer. Answer each question honestly. The credit that is assigned to each response on the actual test is based upon how successful employees described themselves when honestly responding to the questions. *PRINT THE LETTER OF THE CORRECT ANSWER IN THE SPACE AT THE RIGHT.*

1. Generally, in your work assignments, would you prefer   1.____
   A. to work on one thing at a time
   B. to work on a couple of things at a time
   C. to work on many things at the same time

2. In the course of a week, which of the following gives you the GREATEST   2.____
   satisfaction?
   A. Being told you have done a good job.
   B. Helping other people to solve their problems.
   C. Coming up with a new or unique way to handle a situation.
   D. Having free time to devote to personal interests.

EXAMINATION SECTION

TEST 1

DIRECTIONS: Each question or incomplete statement is followed by several suggested answers or completions. Select the one that BEST answers the question or completes the statement. *PRINT THE LETTER OF THE CORRECT ANSWER IN THE SPACE AT THE RIGHT.*

1. While a senior in high school, I was absent
   A. never
   B. seldom
   C. frequently
   D. more than 10 days
   E. only when I felt bored

1._____

2. While in high school, I failed classes
   A. never
   B. once
   C. twice
   D. more than twice
   E. at least four times

2._____

3. During class discussions in my high school classes, I usually
   A. listened without participating
   B. participated as much as possible
   C. listened until I had something to add to the discussion
   D. disagreed with others simply for the sake of argument
   E. laughed at stupid ideas

3._____

4. My high school grade point average (on a 4.0 scale) was
   A. 2.0 or lower
   B. 2.1 to 2.5
   C. 2.6 to 3.0
   D. 3.1 to 3.5
   E. 3.6 to 4.0

4._____

5. As a high school student, I completed my assignments
   A. as close to the due date as I could manage
   B. whenever the teacher gave me an extension
   C. frequently
   D. on time
   E. when they were interesting

5._____

6. While in high school, I participated in
   A. athletic and non-athletic extracurricular activities
   B. athletic extracurricular activities
   C. non-athletic extracurricular activities
   D. no extracurricular activities
   E. mandatory afterschool programs

6._____

7. In high school, I made the honor roll   7._____
   - A. several times
   - B. once
   - C. more than once
   - D. twice
   - E. I cannot remember

8. Upon graduation from high school, I received _____ honors.   8._____
   - A. academic and non-academic
   - B. academic
   - C. non-academic
   - D. no
   - E. I cannot remember

9. While attending high school, I worked at a paid job or as a volunteer   9._____
   - A. never
   - B. every so often
   - C. 5 to 10 hours a month
   - D. more than 10 hours a month
   - E. more than 15 hours a month

10. During my senior year of high school, I skipped school   10._____
    - A. whenever I could
    - B. once a week
    - C. several times a week
    - D. not at all
    - E. when I got bored

11. I was suspended from high school   11._____
    - A. not at all
    - B. once or twice
    - C. once or twice, for fighting
    - D. several times
    - E. more times than I can remember

12. During high school, my fellow students and teachers considered me   12._____
    - A. above average
    - B. below average
    - C. average
    - D. underachieving
    - E. underachieving and prone to fighting

13. An effective leader is someone who   13._____
    - A. inspires confidence in his/her followers
    - B. inspires fear in his/her followers
    - C. tells subordinates exactly what they should do
    - D. creates an environment in which subordinates feel insecure about their job security and performance
    - E. makes as few decisions as possible

14. While a student, I spent my summers and holiday breaks   14._____
    A. in summer or remedial classes
    B. traveling
    C. working
    D. relaxing
    E. spending time with my friends

15. As a high school student, I cut classes   15._____
    A. frequently
    B. when I didn't like them
    C. sometimes
    D. rarely
    E. when I needed the sleep

16. In high school, I received academic honors   16._____
    A. not at all
    B. once
    C. twice
    D. several times
    E. I cannot remember

17. As a student, I failed _____ classes.   17._____
    A. no
    B. two
    C. three
    D. four
    E. more than four

18. Friends describe me as   18._____
    A. introverted
    B. hot-tempered
    C. unpredictable
    D. quiet
    E. easygoing

19. During my high school classes, I preferred to   19._____
    A. remain silent during discussions
    B. do other homework during discussions
    C. participate frequently in discussions
    D. argue with others as much as possible
    E. laugh at the stupid opinions of others

20. As a high school student, I was placed on academic probation   20._____
    A. not at all
    B. once
    C. twice
    D. three times
    E. more than three times

21. At work, being a team player means to   21._____
    A. compromise your ideals and beliefs
    B. compensate for the incompetence of others
    C. count on others to compensate for your inexperience
    D. cooperate with others to get a project finished
    E. rely on others to get the job done

22. My friends from school remember me primarily as a(n)   22._____
    A. person who loved to party
    B. ambitious student
    C. athlete
    D. joker
    E. fighter

23. My school experience is memorable primarily because of   23._____
    A. the friends I made
    B. the sorority/fraternity I was able to join
    C. the social activities I participated in
    D. my academic achievements
    E. the money I spent

24. A friend who is applying for a job asks you to help him pass the   24._____
    mandatory drug test by substituting your urine sample for his. You should
    A. help him by supplying the sample
    B. supply the sample and insist he seek drug counseling
    C. supply the sample, but tell him that this is the only time you'll help
        in this way
    D. call the police
    E. refuse

25. As a student, I handed in my assignments when   25._____
    A. they were due
    B. I could get an extension
    C. they were interesting
    D. my friends reminded me to
    E. I was able to

KEY (CORRECT ANSWERS)

1. A	11. A	21. D
2. A	12. A	22. B
3. C	13. A	23. D
4. E	14. C	24. E
5. D	15. D	25. A
6. A	16. D	
7. A	17. A	
8. A	18. E	
9. E	19. C	
10. D	20. A	

TEST 2

DIRECTIONS: Each question or incomplete statement is followed by several suggested answers or completions. Select the one that BEST answers the question or completes the statement. *PRINT THE LETTER OF THE CORRECT ANSWER IN THE SPACE AT THE RIGHT.*

1. At work you are accused of a minor infraction which you did not commit. Your first reaction is to
   A. call a lawyer
   B. speak to your supervisor about the mistake
   C. call the police
   D. yell at the person who did commit the infraction
   E. accept the consequences regardless of your guilt or innocence

   1._____

2. As a student, I began to prepare for final exams
   A. the night before taking them
   B. when the professor handed out the review sheets
   C. several weeks before taking them
   D. when my friends began to prepare for their exams
   E. the morning of the exam

   2._____

3. At work, I am known as
   A. popular
   B. quiet
   C. intense
   D. easygoing
   E. dedicated

   3._____

4. The most important quality in a coworker is
   A. friendliness
   B. cleanliness
   C. good sense of humor
   D. dependability
   E. good listening skills

   4._____

5. In the past year, I have stayed home from work
   A. frequently
   B. only when I felt depressed
   C. rarely
   D. only when I felt overwhelmed
   E. only to run important errands

   5._____

6. For me, the best thing about school was the
   A. chance to strengthen my friendships and develop new ones
   B. chance to test my abilities and develop new ones
   C. number of extracurricular activities and clubs
   D. chance to socialize
   E. chance to try several different majors

   6._____

7. As an employee, my weakest skill is   7._____
   A. controlling my temper
   B. organizational ability
   C. ability to effectively understand directions
   D. ability to effectively manage others
   E. ability to communicate my thoughts in writing

8. As an employee, my greatest strength would be   8._____
   A. my sense of loyalty
   B. organizational ability
   C. punctuality
   D. dedication
   E. ability to intimidate others

9. If asked by my company to learn a new job-related skill, my reaction   9._____
would be to
   A. ask for a raise
   B. ask for overtime pay
   C. question the necessity of the skill
   D. cooperate with some reluctance
   E. cooperate with enthusiasm

10. When I disagree with others, I tend to   10._____
   A. listen quietly despite my disagreement
   B. laugh openly at the person I disagree with
   C. ask the person to explain their views before I respond
   D. leave the conversation before my anger gets the best of me
   E. point out exactly why the person is wrong

11. When I find myself in a situation which is confusing or unclear, my   11._____
reaction is to
   A. pretend I am not confused
   B. remain calm and, if necessary, ask someone else for clarification
   C. grow frustrated and angry
   D. walk away from the situation
   E. immediately insist that someone explain things to me

12. If you were placed in a supervisory position, which of the following   12._____
abilities would you consider to be most important to your job
performance?
   A. Stubbornness
   B. The ability to hear all sides of a story before making a decision
   C. Kindness
   D. The ability to make and stick to a decision
   E. Patience

13. What is your highest level of education?   13._____
   A. Less than a high school diploma
   B. High school diploma or equivalency
   C. Graduate of community college
   D. Graduate of a four-year accredited college
   E. Degree from graduate school

14. When asked to supervise other workers, your approach should be to   14._____
    A. ask for management wages since you're doing management work
    B. give the workers direction and supervise every aspect of the process
    C. give the workers direction and then allow them to do the job
    D. hand the workers their job specifications
    E. do the work yourself, since you're uncomfortable supervising others

15. Which of the following best describes you?   15._____
    A. Need little or no supervision
    B. Resent too much supervision
    C. Require as much supervision as my peers
    D. Require slightly more supervision than my peers
    E. Require close supervision

16. You accept a job which requires an ability to perform several tasks at once. What is the best way to handle such a position?   16._____
    A. With strong organizational skills and close attention to detail
    B. By delegating the work to someone with strong organizational skills
    C. Staying focused on one task at a time, no matter what happens
    D. Working on one task at a time until each task is successfully completed
    E. Asking your supervisor to help you

17. Which of the following best describes your behavior when you disagree with someone? You   17._____
    A. state your own point of view as quickly and loudly as you can
    B. listen quietly and keep your opinions to yourself
    C. listen to the other person's perspective and then carefully point out all the flaws in their logic
    D. list all of the ignorant people who agree with the opposing point of view
    E. listen to the other person's perspective and then explain your own perspective

18. As a new employee, you make several mistakes during your first week of work. You react by   18._____
    A. learning from your mistakes and moving on
    B. resigning
    C. blaming it on your supervisor
    D. refusing to talk about it
    E. blaming yourself

19. My ability to communicate effectively with others is   19._____
    A. below average
    B. average
    C. above average
    D. far above average
    E. far below average

20. In which of the following areas are you most highly skilled? 20._____
    A. Written communication
    B. Oral communication
    C. Ability to think quickly in difficult situations
    D. Ability to work with a broad diversity of people and personalities
    E. Organizational skills

21. As a worker, you are assigned to work with a partner whom you dislike. 21._____
    You should
    A. immediately report the problem to your supervisor
    B. ask your partner not to speak to you during working hours
    C. tell your colleagues about your differences
    D. tell your partner why you dislike him/her
    E. work with your partner regardless of your personal feelings

22. During high school, what was your most common afterschool activity? 22._____
    A. Remaining after school to participate in various clubs and
       organizations (band, sports, etc.)
    B. Making up for missed classes
    C. Punishment or detention
    D. Going straight to an afterschool job
    E. Spending the afternoon at home or with friends

23. During high school, in which of the following subjects did you receive the 23._____
    highest grades?
    A. English, history, social studies
    B. Math, science
    C. Vocational classes
    D. My grades were consistent in all subjects
    E. Classes I liked

24. When faced with an overwhelming number of duties at work, your 24._____
    reaction is to
    A. do all of the work yourself, no matter what the cost
    B. delegate some responsibilities to capable colleagues
    C. immediately ask your supervisor for help
    D. put off as much work as possible until you can get to it
    E. take some time off to relax and clear your mind

25. Which of the following best describes your desk at your current or most 25._____
    recent job?
    A. Messy and disorganized
    B. Neat and organized
    C. Messy but organized
    D. Neat but disorganized
    E. Messy

KEY (CORRECT ANSWERS)

1. B	11. B	21. E
2. C	12. D	22. A
3. E	13. E	23. D
4. D	14. C	24. B
5. C	15. A	25. B
6. B	16. A	
7. E	17. E	
8. D	18. A	
9. E	19. C	
10. C	20. C	

TEST 3

DIRECTIONS: Each question or incomplete statement is followed by several suggested answers or completions. Select the one that BEST answers the question or completes the statement. *PRINT THE LETTER OF THE CORRECT ANSWER IN THE SPACE AT THE RIGHT.*

1. When asked to take on extra responsibility at work, in order to help out a coworker who is overwhelmed, your response is to
    A. ask for overtime pay
    B. complain to your supervisor that you are being taken advantage of
    C. help the coworker to the best of your ability
    D. ask the coworker to come back some other time
    E. give the coworker some advice on how to get his/her job done

1._____

2. At my last job, I was promoted
    A. not at all
    B. once
    C. twice
    D. three times
    E. more than three times

2._____

3. You are faced with an overwhelming deadline at work. Your reaction is to
    A. procrastinate until the last minute
    B. procrastinate until someone notices that you need some help
    C. notify your supervisor that you cannot complete the work on your own
    D. work in silence without asking any questions
    E. arrange your schedule so that you can get the work done before the deadline

3._____

4. When you feel yourself under deadline pressure at work, your response is
    A. make sure you keep to a schedule which allows you to complete the work on time
    B. wait until just before the deadline to complete the work
    C. ask someone else to do the work
    D. grow so obsessive about the work that your coworkers feel compelled to help you
    E. ask your supervisor immediately for help

4._____

5. Which of the following best describes your appearance at your current or most recent position?
    A. Well-groomed, neat and clean
    B. Unkempt, but dressed neatly
    C. Messy and dirty clothing
    D. Unshaven and untidy
    E. Clean-shaven, but sloppily dressed

5._____

6. Which of the following best describes the way you react to making a 6._____
   difficult decision?
   A. Consult with the people you're closest to before making the
      decision
   B. Make the decision entirely on your own
   C. Consult only with those people whom your decision will affect
   D. Consult with everyone you know, in an effort to make a decision
      that will please everyone
   E. Forget about the decision until you have to make it

7. If placed in a supervisory role, which of the following characteristics would 7._____
   you rely on most heavily when dealing with the employees you
   supervise?
   A. Kindness
   B. Cheeriness
   C. Honesty
   D. Hostility
   E. Aloofness

8. When confronted with gossip at work, your typical reaction is to 8._____
   A. participate
   B. listen without participating
   C. notify your supervisor
   D. excuse yourself from the discussion
   E. confront your coworkers about their problem

9. In the past two years, how many jobs have you held? 9._____
   A. None
   B. One
   C. Two
   D. Three
   E. More than three

10. In your current or most recent job, your favorite part of the job is the part 10._____
    which involves
    A. telling other people what they're doing wrong
    B. supervising others
    C. working without supervision to finish a project
    D. written communication
    E. oral communication

11. Your supervisor asks you about a colleague who is applying for a position 11._____
    which you also want. You react by
    A. commenting honestly on the colleague's work performance
    B. enhancing the person's negative traits
    C. informing your supervisor about your colleague's personal
       problems
    D. telling your supervisor that you would be better in the position
    E. refusing to comment

12. Which of these best describes your responsibilities in your last job?   12._____
    A. Entirely supervisory
    B. Much supervisory responsibility
    C. Equal amounts of supervisory and non-supervisory responsibility
    D. Some supervisory responsibilities
    E. No supervisory responsibilities

13. How much written communication did your previous or most recent job   13._____
require of you?
    A. A great deal
    B. Some
    C. I don't remember
    D. A small amount
    E. None

14. In the past two years, how many times have you been fired from a job?   14._____
    A. None
    B. Once
    C. Twice
    D. Three times
    E. More than three times

15. How many hours per week have you spent working for volunteer   15._____
organizations in the past year?
    A. 10 to 20
    B. 5 to 10
    C. 3 to 5
    D. 1 to 3
    E. None

16. Your efforts at volunteer work usually revolve around which of the   16._____
following types of organizations?
    A. Religious
    B. Community-based organization working to improve the community
    C. Charity on behalf of the poor
    D. Charity on behalf of the infirm or handicapped
    E. Other

17. Which of the following best describes your professional history?   17._____
Promoted at _____ coworkers.
    A. a much faster rate than
    B. a slightly faster rate than
    C. the same rate as
    D. a slightly slower rate than
    E. a much slower rate than

18. Which of the following qualities do you most appreciate in a coworker?   18._____
    A. Friendliness
    B. Dependability
    C. Good looks
    D. Silence
    E. Forgiveness

19. When you disagree with a supervisor's instructions or opinion about how   19._____
to complete a project, your reaction is to
    A. inform your supervisor that you refuse to complete the project
according to his or her instructions
    B. inform your colleagues of your supervisor's incompetence
    C. accept your supervisor's instructions in silence
    D. voice your concerns and then complete the project according to
your own instincts
    E. voice your concerns and then complete the project according to
your supervisor's instructions

20. Which of the following best describes your reaction to close supervision   20._____
and specific direction from your supervisors? You
    A. listen carefully to the direction, then figure out a way to do the job
more effectively
    B. complete the job according to the given specifications
    C. show some initiative by doing the job your way
    D. ask someone else to do the job for you
    E. listen carefully to the directions, and then figure out a better way to
do the job which will save more money

21. At work, you are faced with a difficult decision. You react by   21._____
    A. seeking advice from your colleagues
    B. following your own path regardless of the consequences
    C. asking your supervisor what you should do
    D. keeping the difficulties to yourself
    E. working for a solution which will please everyone

22. If asked to work with a person whom you dislike, your response would be   22._____
    A. to ask your supervisor to allow you to work with someone else
    B. to ask your coworker to transfer to another department or project
    C. talk to your coworker about the proper way to behave at work
    D. pretend the coworker is your best friend for the sake of your job
    E. set aside your personal differences in order to complete the job

23. As a supervisor, which of the following incentives would you use to   23._____
motivate your employees?
    A. Fear of losing their jobs
    B. Fear of their supervisors
    C. Allowing employees to provide their input on a number of policies
    D. Encouraging employees to file secret reports regarding
colleagues' transgressions
    E. All of the above

24. A fellow worker, with whom you enjoy a close friendship, has a substance abuse problem which has gone undetected. You suspect the problem may be affecting his job. You would
    A. ask the worker if the problem is affecting his job performance
    B. warn the worker that he must seek counseling or you will report him
    C. wait a few weeks to see whether the worker's problem really is affecting his job
    D. discuss it with your supervisor
    E. wait for the supervisor to discover the problem

24._____

25. In the past two months, you have missed work
    A. never
    B. once
    C. twice
    D. three times
    E. more than three times

25._____

KEY (CORRECT ANSWERS)

1. C	11. A	21. A
2. C	12. D	22. E
3. E	13. B	23. C
4. A	14. A	24. D
5. A	15. C	25. A
6. A	16. B	
7. C	17. A	
8. D	18. B	
9. B	19. E	
10. C	20. B	

CPSIA information can be obtained
at www.ICGtesting.com
Printed in the USA
LVHW060639150719

624058LV00012B/160/P